ENCORE!
MORE WINNING
MONOLOGS
for
YOUNG ACTORS

*63 more honest-to-life monologs
for teenage boys and girls*

PEG KEHRET

MERIWETHER PUBLISHING LTD.
Colorado Springs, Colorado

Meriwether Publishing Ltd., Publisher
PO Box 7710
Colorado Springs, CO 80933-7710

Editor: Arthur L. Zapel
Cover design: Michelle Z. Gallardo

Library of Congress Cataloging-in-Publication Data

Kehret, Peg.
    Encore! : more winning monologs for young actors.

    Summary: A collection of monologs for use in junior high and high school drama classes.
    1. Acting — Juvenile literature. 2. Monologues — Juvenile literature. [1. Acting. 2. Monologues]
I. Title.
PN2080.K34   1988   812'.54   88-42541
ISBN 13: 978-0-916260-54-5
ISBN 10: 0-916260-54-2

For Kevin Konen
My son-in-heart

TABLE OF CONTENTS

Part One:

MONOLOGS FOR GIRLS

Part Two:

MONOLOGS FOR BOYS

Part Three:

MONOLOGS FOR BOYS OR GIRLS

Part One:

MONOLOGS FOR GIRLS

A Curse Upon You, Sister
Mom Always Liked Her Best
Bald Is Beautiful
Drill Team Try-Outs
Ghosts and Ghoulies and Bad Big Brothers
Vicki Might Have Been President
The Peanut Butter and Spider Sandwich
Leg Shaving Made Easy
Like Mom, Like Kid
Kathy's Pregnant
Footsteps in the Night
Class Pictures
You Put **What** on Your Hair?
Getting My First Bra
In 100 Years, Who'll Know the Difference?
Double Trouble
How I Quit Biting My Fingernails
Garbage Gifts

A Curse Upon You, Sister

I once put a curse on my sister. I didn't make a voodoo doll out of my sister's hair and then stick pins in it, or anything like that. I didn't want Ellie to die or even to get hurt. All I wanted was for her to quit borrowing my clothes.

Nothing infuriated me so much as going to my closet, intending to wear my brown sweater, only to find that Ellie had beat me to it and that my brown sweater was, at that very moment, riding on Ellie's shoulders to a high school football game.

When she got home, I confronted her and demanded to know why she took my brown sweater without permission. She gave me that sickening wide-eyed-innocent look that she always gives our grandpa. Then she swore that she tried to ask permission but I was nowhere around and so she just assumed that since I wasn't home, I wouldn't be needing the brown sweater.

What she really did was to wait until I was gone and then sneak the sweater out of my closet, hoping she could put it back before I noticed it was missing. Every time I caught Ellie wearing something of mine without permission, it made me wonder how many times she took things that I never found out about.

Once, when I went to put on my blue and white striped blouse, I found a smudge on the sleeve. I knew I had washed and ironed that blouse after I wore it last, so I accused Ellie of wearing it, getting it dirty, and hanging it back in the closet.

She denied everything. She denied it so vehemently that I began to question my own memory. I backed down and apologized for accusing her. Two days later, Ellie's friend, Barbara, came over. Barbara had snapshots of her birthday party and she showed them to me while she waited for Ellie to get home. Guess what Ellie was wearing in the pictures. That's right. My blue and white striped blouse. The one she swore had never touched her skin.

It didn't do any good to complain to Mom. All she said was that we each had plenty and could afford to share.

I decided drastic measures were necessary. First I tried to lock my closet door but it's a sliding door and I couldn't figure out how to attach a lock to it.

Then I considered constructing some kind of booby trap that would go off when the door was opened. Specifically, I thought I might rig up a big pan of cooked spaghetti that would dump on the head of anyone who opened the closet door. The trouble with that plan was if someone other than Ellie opened the door — like my mother, for example — I might be in big trouble. Also, I didn't want cold spaghetti all over my floor.

My solution, as I said, was to put a curse on my sister. I didn't know anything about curses so I got a book about magic from the library. It told some of the rituals that witches use. In most of them, the witch held an animal bone in one hand and a photograph of the victim in the other hand while she repeated a magic chant.

The photograph was no problem. I already had one of Ellie's school pictures. The bone was easy, too. I told Mom I would cook dinner if it could be fried chicken. Mom will agree to almost any menu if one of us will do the cooking. I cooked chicken and saved the bone from the drumstick.

The chant took awhile. Writing is not my strong suit and I wanted the chant to be good. I did twelve revisions before I was satisfied.

I held Ellie's picture in one hand and the chicken bone in the other while I said my chant:

> If you take clothes
> That aren't your own,
> Sneaky sister,
> You will moan. You will groan.
> Sister, you will moan and groan.

I was so pleased with how the chant sounded that I repeated it seven times. I was sure it would work. I was *so* sure that I wanted to be there when it did, to see exactly what would happen.

I began staking out my closet. I lingered in the bathroom with my ear to the door, hoping to hear Ellie go into my room. I hid under my bed for two hours. While I waited, I kept wondering what would happen to make Ellie moan and groan. Would the closet door jump off its track and run over Ellie's foot? Would the borrowed piece of clothing snag her hair and refuse to become untangled? It was dusty under the bed and I had to keep stifling sneezes. Maybe Ellie heard me and that's why she didn't come into my room.

The next night after dinner I sat in the closet with the door shut and my bathrobe draped over my head so Ellie wouldn't see me when she opened the door. I sat there the entire evening and missed all of my favorite television shows. Ellie didn't come.

I hung around my room for two weeks, trying to catch Ellie in the act. Finally I couldn't stand it any longer and I asked her why she never borrowed my clothes any more.

"Because they're too babyish," she said. "I prefer something more sophisticated."

"Like *my* new green blouse," Mom said. "I had planned to wear it to work today and when I went to put it on, it was gone."

I said, "Mom, you have plenty of clothes. You can afford to share."

Mom glared at me. Then she gave Ellie a lecture about asking permission to use other people's things *and* she said if Ellie ever did it again, she'd be grounded.

Ellie moaned.

Ellie groaned.

My curse had worked.

#2

Mom Always Liked Her Best

All through my childhood, I knew that my mother liked my sister, Angie, best. For one thing, Angie has naturally curly hair. I either had to wear my hair in braids, which looked babyish, or else Mom would give me home permanents, an ordeal which she seemed to hate almost as much as I did. There I sat, with a terrycloth towel around my shoulders and my eyes squeezed shut as tight as I could, trying to hold my nose without making the towel fall off.

Mom always said things like, "Sit still, Virginia. I have to get this neutralizer on evenly." At least once during the ordeal, she would say, "If only you had hair like Angie's."

Angie would waltz through the kitchen with her curls bouncing and say, "Ugh! You're going to stink like a skunk." And I couldn't even jump up and whack her.

Then there were the gymnastics lessons. Angie and I begged to take gymnastics lessons, so twice a week, Mom drove us to the local YWCA. She sat in a corner of the gym and read a book or did her knitting while Angie and I learned to do roundoff back handsprings and front aerials. That is, Angie learned to do round-off back handsprings and front aerials. I never progressed beyond cartwheels.

Try as I might, I just never had the agility or coordination to do the stunts that the other girls did. I was a klutz, on or off the exercise mat. I'll never forget the day the gymnastics coach suggested to Mom that I no longer work on the balance beam. He said he couldn't give adequate attention to the other girls when he had to stand beside the beam all the time, waiting to catch me when I fell off. The real clincher was when he said, "It isn't fair to the girls like Angie, who have some natural talent."

And do you know what Mom said? She agreed with him.

Secretly, I was kind of relieved not to have to get up on that balance beam any more. It's no fun to be four feet off the floor, trying to do somersaults and pirouette turns.

I couldn't do those well when I was on solid ground, much less when I was tottering on that narrow little beam. Still, even though I was glad to be done with the balance beam, I was sorry that Mom didn't argue with the coach, even a little bit. It was just one more example of how she always liked Angie best.

When Angie was in sixth grade and I was in fourth grade, we started music lessons. Angie took piano and I took violin. After only a few weeks of lessons, Angie's music teacher called Mom to report that Angie was one of those gifted individuals who could play music by ear. She could pick out tunes, without having any printed music in front of her.

When Grandma and Grandpa came to visit, they asked Angie to "play a little tune" for them and then Grandma and Grandpa clapped and Mom told them all about the phone call from Angie's music teacher. Mom doesn't play an instrument and she sounded kind of awe struck when she told about Angie.

My violin lessons were OK, except that every time I practiced, our Cocker Spaniel howled. Mom said it was because the high notes hurt his ears. Angie said the notes hurt her ears, too, and not just the high ones. Mom suggested that I practice in my bedroom, with the door closed.

I said Angie didn't have to practice in *her* bedroom with the door closed and Mom said that was because it wasn't possible to move a heavy piano into the bedroom. But I knew better. I knew that Mom didn't like to hear me practice any more than Snooper did, because Mom really liked Angie the best.

Last week Angie left for college. She got a scholarship, of course. Mom cried when Angie left and I felt kind of weepy myself. Angie and I were never best pals, the way some sisters are, but we never had any major fights, either. The house seems different now. Empty.

Yesterday when I got home, Mom was standing in front of

the mirror, brushing her hair furiously and cursing her hairdresser. I didn't blame her. Her head looked like a Brillo™ pad.

"I *told* him I didn't want a tight perm," Mom said. "I told him just a body wave, just soft curls. And look at this!" She yanked at a fistful of hair, so hard I thought she was going to pull it out.

I felt sorry for her. I suggested that we wet her hair and roll it on huge rollers to straighten it out. I told her I sometimes do that when my perms are too tight.

Mom agreed to try it. She said she knew I'd understand, because I'm so much like her. Then she said — and I could not believe what I was hearing — she said that's probably why I've always been her favorite. She said we're so much alike, with our straight hair and our klutziness and our lack of special talent, and that's why she's always liked me best.

#3

Bald Is Beautiful

Did you ever think about how important hair is? It's the first thing mentioned when anyone describes another person. She's blond, they'll say; or, he's a redhead.

Shampoo ads make it seem like a person's hair is the *only* important thing about them. As long as your hair is shiny, bouncy and free of dandruff, you have no problems.

With so much emphasis on hair, it's small wonder that I came unglued when I found out I was going to lose mine.

I didn't cry when I had the CAT scan. I didn't cry when the doctor told me about the brain tumor. But after I found out I had to have my head shaved, I cried.

My mom said my hair would grow back and my dad said I could buy a wig and my little brother, Syd, said think how much time I would save in the bathroom every morning.

My sister, Janie, was the only one who understood. She said it was terrible that I had to be bald and she didn't blame me one bit for crying.

The surgery went even better than expected. The tumor was small and it was not malignant. When I woke up, I was weak and woozy, but for the first time in months, I didn't have a headache.

But when I looked in the mirror, I almost threw up. I looked like one of those mannequin heads that beauty shops display wigs on. I was smooth and white and round. And ugly. I never saw anything so ugly as me with no hair.

At my second checkup, the doctor removed the stitches and said I could go back to school half days. I was scheduled to start the next Monday afternoon.

I didn't want to go. I looked like a freak. How could I go back to school, looking like a freak? Even if I wore a wig, everyone would know it was a wig and stare at me. What if the wig fell off? What if some creepy boy pulled it off? I said I would rather dance barefoot in a barrel of thistles than go back to school without any hair on my head.

I told my parents that if I had to go back to school bald, I would run away and sleep in a cave and eat wild berries. They said I couldn't sit around and feel sorry for myself and do nothing but wait for my hair to grow out. My mother said if I didn't want to wear a wig to school, I could wear a turban. I said a turban would be even worse than a wig and I refused to get either one. My father said I should be thankful I was alive and to quit complaining about my lack of hair.

Syd asked me to go to his homeroom on my first day back, because he'd bet some kid fifty cents that his sister was bald and he wanted to collect his money.

Janie didn't say anything.

I said I would be a freak for the next six months and I would never be happy again until I got my hair back.

My dad said to quit calling myself a freak and I said one bald girl in the whole school was most definitely a freak.

When Janie and Syd left for school on Monday morning, Syd started to remind me about his fifty-cent bet, until Janie poked him and told him to be quiet.

The minutes dragged by that morning. I dreaded walking into the school and having everyone stare at me. I dreaded being different from all the other kids. I never felt more alone than I did that morning while I waited until it was time to go. I was miserable and I knew when I got to school, I'd be even more miserable.

I couldn't eat any lunch. I sat at the table, staring at my cheese sandwich and waiting for Janie. I had asked her to come home at noon and go back with me, so I wouldn't have to walk into the school that first time alone. Maybe she wouldn't come. She probably decided she didn't want to be seen with a freak. Who could blame her?

I tried not to cry. It was bad enough to be bald; I didn't want my eyes to be all red and swollen, too.

I heard the front door open.

Behind me, I heard Janie say, "Are you ready to go?"

I swallowed hard, trying to get up my courage.

"The way I figure it," she went on, "Syd's friend owes him a dollar."

I started to say there was no way I was going to parade my bald head around in front of Syd's friends, and then I turned and saw her.

Janie had skipped class that morning. Instead of going to school, she went downtown and got her head shaved. She was smooth, and white, and round, just like me.

I sat still as stone, while the full impact of what she had done sank in.

"One bald girl might be a freak," she told me. "Two bald girls could start a new fashion."

Although the words were joking, her lip quivered as she spoke.

When we got to school, everyone stared, just like I knew they would. But I wasn't miserable. I wasn't miserable at all. I was happy! As I marched down the hall with my head held high, and my beautiful sister beside me, I knew that some things are way more important than hair.

#4

Drill Team Try-Outs

When I started junior high school, my main ambition in life was to be a member of the school Drill Team. The Drill Team members wore special short red skirts and gold sweaters and they performed during half time at the football and basketball games. On game days, they wore their uniforms to class and got excused a half hour early. They didn't have to pay to get in to the games, which cost the rest of us one dollar. Sometimes they even got to take a school bus to games at other schools, and they got in free there, too. In my eyes, the Drill Team members were the luckiest people in the world.

I told my best friend, Jessica, about my desire to be on the Drill Team. I said I intended to make up a routine and practice it every day so that when Drill Team auditions were held, I'd be ready.

Jessica didn't want to try out for Drill Team because she plays clarinet in the school band and the band practices after school, at the same time as Drill Team practice.

I did make up a routine. It took me weeks to choose a song I liked and weeks more to put together a routine to go with the song. Eventually, I had one that I thought was good enough. I practiced it every day after school and again in the evening until my parents made me quit. They said if they had to listen to that same music one more time, they would go crazy. After that, I practiced with my earphones on.

By the time Drill Team auditions were announced, I was as ready as it was possible for me to be. On the day of the try-outs, I felt confident. I'd practiced so much, I knew there was no way I'd forget my routine.

I didn't get nervous until I walked into the gymnasium and saw how many other girls were trying out. It looked like the entire school was there. Some of them wore short red skirts and gold sweaters, which made them seem like they already belonged on the team. I wished I'd thought of that. My brown slacks and tan and white striped top seemed tacky in comparison.

One group of girls sat together and cheered for each other. As each of their names was called, the whole group whistled and clapped and the one who was trying out would smile and wave at them.

My stomach began to churn as I watched the polished, complicated routines that some of the girls did. My routine, which I had worked so hard to create and practiced so diligently, began to seem babyish.

Finally, my name was called. When I stood up, I heard someone clapping like crazy. I looked up and saw Jessica in the stands. She had skipped band practice to come and cheer for me.

I got through my routine with no mistakes but I had no idea whether it was good enough to make the team or not. A list of those who made it would be posted the next morning.

I got to school early the next day and headed straight for the gym. The list was there, but my name wasn't on it. I wanted to crawl into a hole and cry. All those hours and hours of practice, and I didn't make the team.

The people who did make the team were all screaming and jumping around. Some of them got flowers from their friends, to congratulate them.

When I got to my first class, there was a pink carnation on my desk. The note with it said, "Congratulations on being a wonderful friend." I recognized Jessica's handwriting.

As I pinned the carnation to my sweater, I thought about Jessica and a grin spread across my face. I felt like the luckiest person in the world, even if I wasn't on the Drill Team.

#5

Ghosts and Ghoulies and Bad Big Brothers

Until I was seven years old, I was afraid of the dark. I believed that horrible creatures crouched behind my bedroom door and hid under my bed, awaiting their chance to pounce.

My bedroom was on the second floor of our house. Since I was the youngest, I had to go to bed first, which meant that I was supposed to go up the dark stairs and turn on the light. Once the light was on, I wasn't frightened. But until the light was turned on, I was petrified. Each night, as I reached for the light switch on the wall, I was sure that before my hand could find it, the ghosts and ghoulies would get me.

Because of my fear, one of my parents climbed the stairs with me, and turned on the light for me, every night. The older I got, the more they resented this unnecessary drain on their time and energies. Even when they armed me with a flashlight, it didn't help; each night I demanded an escort.

Finally my mother embarked on a campaign designed to cure me of my fear. She set a date: March first. She gave me a pep talk about how grown-up I was and then suggested that by the time March first came around, I would be so grown-up that I would be able to go upstairs by myself at night and get ready for bed. All alone. She used her most persuasive voice; she even offered a reward in the form of an increase in my allowance after I successfully accomplished the goal. I was apprehensive at first but I agreed to try.

That's when the serious advertising blitz began. No new product ever had a bigger build-up than my impending trip up the stairs alone.

Mother enthusiastically told everyone who came to our house that on March first, I was going to go to bed by myself.

My father echoed her statements. Even my brother, Fred, who is six years older than I and who thought the whole situation was stupid, was coerced into commenting that I was brave. He said it with a snicker, but he did say it.

When March first was only one week away, the grand countdown began. Every night, as Mother and I climbed the stairs, she built more suspense for the big event. "One week from tonight, you'll be so grown-up you'll do this all by yourself." "Six days from now, you won't need me with you anymore." "Only five more days until you go to bed all alone."

By the time March first arrived, the brainwashing was complete and I was convinced that I could do it. I intended to march up the stairs, enter my dark room alone, and turn on the light. Excited about my impending triumph, I was actually eager for my bedtime to arrive.

With my parents at the foot of the stairs, urging me on, I embarked on my climb. Up I went, filled with confidence. I reached the top, glanced briefly back at my cheering squad, and strode purposefully toward my room.

I got to the doorway. I groped for the light switch. As my hand neared the switch, Fred sprang out of the closet, with a white sheet draped over his head.

"AAAeeeiigghhhh!!" he shouted. He waved his arms up and down so that the sheet billowed out, seeming to float above my head in the darkness.

I screamed and fled back down the stairs. I flung myself into Mother's arms, sobbing and shaking. It's probably a good thing I did, because if Mother's hands had been free, I suspect she would have strangled Fred on the spot.

As it was, Dad hauled him down the stairs, with the sheet still draped around his shoulders, and made him apologize to me. He lost his allowance for a month and had to do dishes by himself for two weeks, instead of alternating nights with me like we usually did.

When I saw how angry my parents were, I stopped crying

and smirked a bit. Fred was always playing tricks on me and usually he got away with it. I rarely had the pleasure of seeing him get in big trouble because of something he did to me.

The strange result of the March First Bedtime Ghost Disaster, as my father referred to it, was that I did lose my fear of the dark. I'm not sure if it was because Mother's brainwashing was so thorough that it worked despite my brother, or if seeing Fred in the sheet somehow convinced me that all ghosts and goblins are only make-believe. Whatever the reason, from then on I was unafraid. I was able to climb the stairs alone at night and turn on the light without a moment of fear.

I didn't let anyone know of my new-found courage for several weeks, though. Every night, I pretended to be scared. Every night, my parents got mad at Fred all over again. It was wonderful.

#6

Vicki Might Have Been President

I heard what Vicki said but I didn't think she meant it. All kids say things like that sometimes. I've said them myself: "I'd rather die than take that history test." Or, "If I have to babysit my stupid brother one more time, I'm going to kill myself." But even though I sometimes say things like that, I don't really mean them. Not literally. I might complain a lot about babysitting but I'd never do anything drastic. I certainly would never commit suicide.

Vicki did. When she said her life was so gross that it wasn't worth living, she really meant it. I wonder if things might have turned out differently if I had taken her seriously. I wonder how many other people heard her say her life wasn't worth living and assumed, like I did, that she was only exaggerating.

How do you tell when somebody's just letting off steam, or when they're really depressed? When I said if I had to babysit one more time I would kill myself, I was just complaining, just mouthing off so my parents would feel guilty and pay me, instead of expecting me to always babysit for free. But when Vicki told me her life was so gross she was going to kill herself, she was telling it straight.

I'd give anything in the world if I could go back and have that conversation with her again. Why didn't I ask her what it was about her life that was so gross? Maybe she had a problem that I could have helped with, if I had known what it was. Why didn't I tell her that I liked her a lot and wanted to be her friend? Why didn't I at least make sure if she was kidding or not? If I had known she wasn't, I could have told my mom or one of the teachers or some other person who might have been able to help.

Instead, when Vicki said she was going to kill herself, I didn't believe she really meant it. Rather than recognizing her cry for help and reaching out to her, I said, "Yeah, I know what you mean. My life's gross, too." Some answer. A fat lot of help I was.

They found Vicki's body the next morning. When our principal announced her death, I got sick to my stomach and had to go home.

If only I had listened — really listened — to Vicki. If only I had cared enough to be sure whether she was serious or not. Think of the difference I might have made!

Vicki would probably have gone on to college. She got good grades; people liked her. She might have become a teacher or an architect or a lawyer. Maybe she would have written beautiful poetry or invented a fun new game. We'll never know what special talents got buried with Vicki.

The worst part of all is knowing that if Vicki had only waited and sought help, her life would not have looked so bleak. She could have been happy.

I'll never again make a joke about killing myself, no matter how often I have to babysit my stupid brother for free. That kind of remark isn't funny any more.

I listen differently now, too. I try to hear what people are really saying and if I'm not sure I understand, I ask questions.

I won't get a second chance with Vicki. No matter how much I wish I could go back in time and respond differently when she says her life is gross, it isn't possible. All I can do is remember her and try to be sure that any other Vicki in the world gets help when she needs it.

Why am I telling you all this? So that when your friends talk to you, you'll pay attention. Don't make the mistake I made.

Listen.

#7

The Peanut Butter and Spider Sandwich

When I went to Girl Scout camp, I took along a survival kit. It contained peanut butter, crackers and Hershey™ bars, in case they served liver for lunch.

The bathroom at camp was down a trail and through some trees — a small wooden building with a distinctive odor.

I didn't mind the smell. I did mind the spiders who lived there.

The camp counselors sprayed with bug bombs but either the spiders were so hardy that they survived the spray, or there was an endless supply of spiders and when we killed off one, another simply moved in to take its place. I suspect there was a waiting list of spiders who wanted to live in that outhouse.

I always put off going to the bathroom. When I couldn't wait any longer, I would rush down the path, dash inside, and stand perfectly still while I surveyed every inch of the walls, ceiling, and floor. I had to locate the spiders so that I could watch them the entire time I was inside. My worst fear was that a spider would crawl up my leg when I wasn't looking.

A girl at camp named Angel always bragged about her rich family. The only good thing about Angel was her purple jacket, which was the most beautiful coat I'd ever seen.

One night Angel said her father would send her money any time she asked him to. She said he gave her as much as she wanted, even if she didn't say why she wanted it.

I said I doubted that her father would send her one hundred dollars if she didn't tell him why she wanted it. Angel said he would. I said, "I bet he won't."

And Angel said, "What do you want to bet?"

I thought fast. I said, "If he doesn't send you the hundred

dollars, you have to give me your purple jacket."

Angel's eyes narrowed. "OK," she said. "But if he *does* send me a hundred dollars, you have to eat one of the spiders out of the bathroom."

I hesitated. There was no way I could eat one of those spiders, not even for Angel's purple jacket. On the other hand, I was positive nobody's father would send one hundred dollars without knowing what it was for. He couldn't be *that* rich. If he was, Angel would be at some fancy private camp, with indoor bathrooms.

I said it was a deal. We put our hands on our hearts and vowed, "Scout's honor."

I looked around the campfire. A circle of wide-eyed faces stared back at me, witnesses to my promise.

Angel called her father. Six kids listened, to be sure she didn't give him any reason for wanting the money.

Three days later, Angel received a money order for one hundred dollars. She waved it under my nose. In the other hand she clutched a plastic bag containing a large, black spider. "Here's your lunch," she said, as she handed me the plastic bag.

I looked at the spider. It was trying to crawl around the inside of the bag. I dropped the bag. Angel smiled. A huge group of girls clustered around to watch.

I took a deep breath, picked up the bag, and started walking toward the camp kitchen, holding the bag at arm's length.

When Angel realized where I was going, she screeched, "You can't cook it! That's not fair. Nobody said anything about cooking it."

"The bet was for me to eat the spider," I replied. "Nobody said it had to be eaten raw."

Fortunately, the other kids agreed with me. I trudged slowly toward the kitchen, trying to think how I could camouflage the spider enough that I could choke it down. Maybe I could roll the spider in cracker crumbs and fry it in butter. If I put enough salt and pepper on it, it might taste OK. I hoped the cook had plenty of ketchup.

When we got to the kitchen, the cook refused to let us in. She said it was against the rules for the campers to do any cooking. Something about the camp's insurance.

I'd given my Scout's honor that I would eat the spider. I couldn't go back on my word. But I knew I couldn't pop that spider into my mouth plain, either. My stomach lurched at the thought.

Then I remembered my survival kit. The Hershey℠ bars were long gone but I still had some crackers and peanut butter. I spread a thick layer of peanut butter on two of the crackers. I opened the plastic bag and, holding a cracker in my hand, reached inside. Quickly, I smashed the spider into the peanut butter and put the two crackers together with the peanut butter and the spider in the middle. I don't know if he was dead or not; I couldn't stand to look.

I held the world's first peanut-butter-and-spider sandwich for five minutes while I worked up my courage. Then I stuffed it in my mouth and tried to swallow it whole but it wouldn't go down. I had to chew it.

To be honest, it didn't taste much different than crackers and peanut butter always taste. If I hadn't known there was a spider inside, I would have had no problem. But I knew. Did I ever know! It was all I could think about. I bit as gingerly as I could and mushed everything around inside my mouth, trying to keep it off my tongue. My hands felt clammy. I held my nose, squeezed my eyes tight shut, and gulped. Everything stuck in my throat. I gulped again.

Finally, it went down. I got to keep Angel's purple jacket but I have never worn it. Every time I put it on, I think about spiders.

#8

Leg Shaving Made Easy

The first time I noticed that most women have smooth legs while most men have hairy legs, I thought it was an act of Nature. I thought when I became an adult, I, too, would have smooth lovely legs. It didn't occur to me until my own legs began to resemble a chimpanzee that it was necessary to give Nature an assist.

I asked my friend Cheryl about it and she told me that women must shave their legs, just like men shave their faces. She said women usually shave their armpits, too. It was news to me but I figured Cheryl must know, since her legs were nice and smooth. Although I'd never seen her armpits, I was willing to take her word for it.

I didn't ask Cheryl for any instructions on *how* to shave because she was already looking at me as if she thought my IQ was in the minus department for not knowing that women shave their legs. I wasn't about to ask her any more stupid questions.

Besides, I figured shaving is shaving. You hold a razor in your hand and run it across your skin and the hair disappears. Nothing to it.

I was in a hurry to grow up and I figured here was one sure way to instantly look more adult. All I had to do was shave my legs and my armpits.

I didn't have a razor but my dad had one in the bathroom. I got it and sat down on the edge of the bathtub, with my foot up on the sink. I put the razor on my ankle and pulled it up toward my knee.

If I had asked Cheryl HOW to shave my legs, she might have told me that I needed to use soap suds or shaving cream or some other product to soften the hair and make the razor glide easily. But I didn't ask. And I had no soap or shaving cream. I used nothing, not even water. I just put the razor on my dry, hairy leg and yanked.

It was not a pleasant sensation. The razor blade cut the hairs off but I wondered if it might not be easier to pluck them, one at a time.

My skin turned red and itched. The edge of the blade got clogged with dry hair. I nicked myself five times and had to stick little wet blobs of toilet tissue on my leg to stop the bleeding. Once started, though, I had to continue. I couldn't very well have one smooth leg and one hairy one.

I did stop at my knees. I decided my thighs wouldn't show unless I wore shorts and there was no point torturing myself more than necessary. I tried rubbing hand lotion on my legs. It helped the itching and made them sting instead.

After I finished shaving my legs, I planned to shave under my arms. I raised one arm, held the razor in place, and gritted my teeth. I paused and looked down at my raw, itching legs. I wondered if Cheryl had told me the truth about the armpits. I decided to wait a few years to grow up completely.

#9

Like Mom, Like Kid

My mother is the only person I know who truly does not care what other people think. She isn't selfish, or unkind. She just makes up her own mind about everything without regard for such matters as fashion or social trends. A mother like that can be embarrassing.

For example, my mother is probably the only woman in the civilized world who refuses to have her ears pierced. She says she doesn't see any reason to mutilate her body in order to be fashionable. Last week when Mom was having her hair cut, the hairdresser exclaimed, "You don't have pierced ears!" and everyone in the whole beauty shop turned to stare.

It didn't bother my mother at all. She says she doesn't care what the hairdresser thinks. It bothered me, though. I didn't like everyone staring at my mom, as if she were some kind of freak.

I love my mother but I *do* care what other people think and as a result, I'm sometimes embarrassed to be in public with her. I never know what she's going to do next.

We went to a baseball game one night and when someone on our team hit a home run, my mother put her fingers in her mouth and whistled through her teeth. I jumped about two feet. Talk about loud!

That's the kind of thing she does. My dad says that's why he loves her; he says he never gets bored. It's true; my mom is not boring.

She entered a contest that was put on by our local newspaper. People were supposed to write what their secret fantasy was and then the newspaper made the five winner's fantasies come true. Mom was one of the winners.

Everyone else wrote in stuff like they wanted to shake hands with the Governor or have a maid for a day. Not Mom. Do you know what her secret fantasy was? She wanted to feed the lions at the zoo! She did it, too. She even got her picture in the paper, as she stepped into the lions' cage with a bucket of raw meat. The lions' trainer was so impressed that he offered to let Mom go back in the cage with him, after the lions ate, so that she could pet one of them. We have a picture hanging in our den that shows Mom petting an enormous lion and I swear Mom doesn't even look nervous. She says the lion was just an oversized pussycat.

Last summer we had a heat wave that lasted nearly three weeks. The temperatures were in the nineties, day after day, and the water company rationed water. You could only water your lawn on certain days, depending on your house numbers.

Most mothers, under such conditions, would sit in the house in front of a fan and sip iced tea. My mom came home from work, put on her swimsuit, and ran through the sprinkler. She said since it was our day to water the lawn, we should make double use of the water.

It wouldn't have been so bad if she had done it in the back yard. But our back yard is mostly a wooden deck, so there was Mom, right out in front for the whole world to see, running through the sprinkler.

What if some of my friends came over and saw Mom acting like a little kid? They would think she was crazy.

I stayed inside but it was hotter in the house than it was outdoors. I sat by the window, hoping for a little breeze. None came. I looked out at Mom. She was dashing back and forth through the water, laughing and waving at Mrs. Clifton, who lives next door. Pretty soon little Joey Clifton, who's about four, came over and asked if he could run through our sprinklers, too.

It didn't look so bad, once Joey came. It looked like Mom was just there to supervise him. I sat at the window and thought about that. Why is it socially unacceptable for a grown woman to run through the sprinklers alone but perfectly all right for her to do it when there's a child with her? I realized my feelings didn't make sense.

I also realized that I was sitting in the sweltering house feeling hot and sticky and crabby while Mom and Joey were laughing and racing through the cool water.

I put on my swimsuit and went outside. I looked around to see if anyone was watching.

When Mom saw me, she yelled, "Come on in, the water's fine!" And it was.

We were playing Sprinkler Frisbe when two of my friends walked down our street. They looked shocked to see me acting like a little kid but I didn't care. I was having too much fun to worry about what anybody else thought.

#10

Kathy's Pregnant

My sister is pregnant. My sister, Kathy. Sixteen years old and she has managed to completely mess up her life.

She told me last night. She wants me to be with her when she tells Mom and Dad. I couldn't believe my ears when she told me. How could she be so stupid? How could she possibly let herself get pregnant? It isn't as if she'd never been told how to prevent it. She took the Health Ed. class at school last year and Mom's lectured us since we were twelve years old about not having sex because we might get pregnant or get AIDS or just get hurt by some guy who says he loves us. Mom even told us we could go to Planned Parenthood if we didn't want to talk to her or Dr. Johns about it. But did Kathy do it? No. She listened to all the advice and then she went right ahead as if she didn't know anything at all.

"Why didn't you make him wear a condom?" I asked her. "Why would you take such a chance?"

Do you know what she said? My supposedly bright sister, who has a three-point-seven-five grade average, said, "I thought Jeff would take care of that."

She never even asked him!

She's going to tell Mom and Dad tonight. Dad will have a heart attack for sure. I don't even want to think about it. When Dad finds out that his precious Kathy, his darling little girl, is pregnant, I swear he will have a heart attack. I told Kathy to keep the telephone close by because we'll have to call the aid car when Dad hears this.

She didn't want to tell them yet. She wanted to wait until she shows, but I said, no way. The sooner they know, the better, and it won't be any easier to tell them a couple of months from now. Dad's going to have an attack either way, and as for Mom,

I can't even imagine what she will say. She won't blow her stack the way Dad will, but she'll probably cry and that's almost worse. I've only seen Mom cry once — I mean, *really* cry, not just tears at a sad movie — and that was when my grandpa died. Mom cried all that day and it was awful. I told Kathy she'd better be prepared for Mom to cry again tonight.

First Kathy told me she and Jeff would probably get married. But when I asked her *when,* and where they were going to live, I could tell from the look on her face that Jeff is skipping out on her. So much for true love.

What a mess. Kathy's eyes were practically swollen shut last night. And what will this do to her education? With her grades, we always thought she'd have a chance for a college scholarship. Now she'll be lucky to finish high school.

How could Kathy be so stupid? How could my sister be so stupid?

#11

Footsteps in the Night

My first babysitting job was for the Athens family, who live across the street from us. When Mrs. Athens asked me if I ever did babysitting, I told her, "Sure, I do it all the time," and then I went straight home and asked Ma if I could babysit.

Ma said it was OK as long as she and Pa were home, just in case something went wrong.

I told her nothing could go wrong.

Mrs. Athens told me to come at seven-thirty and I was there right on time. The baby, Jessica, was already asleep. Mrs. Athens told me that Jessica would probably stay asleep the whole time I was there, but that if she woke up, there was a bottle in the refrigerator.

After Mr. and Mrs. Athens left, I tiptoed into Jessica's room and looked at her. She was lying on her stomach with her rear end up in the air, making little snuffling sounds against the sheet. She seemed awfully small and I hoped I wouldn't have to feed her the bottle of milk. I wasn't sure I knew how to pick her up.

I wandered back into the living room and leafed through some magazines. Mrs. Athens had said it was OK to watch TV, but I was afraid that if I turned on the TV, I wouldn't hear Jessica if she woke up.

I was reading all the short funny pieces in *The Reader's Digest* when I heard the footsteps. They came from directly over me, from the upstairs of the Athens' house. I held my breath and listened. Someone was up there. Someone was walking around in the room directly over my head.

I reached for the phone to call Ma. But if I talked on the telephone, whoever was upstairs would hear me and know I was there.

Probably whoever it was had seen Mr. and Mrs. Athens

leave and assumed that no one was home. It was the perfect time to steal all the silverware and the family jewels. The burglar probably came in while I was in Jessica's room. What would he do if I announced my presence by talking on the telephone? I decided not to take the chance.

I crept quietly into the kitchen and took a butcher knife out of a drawer. I carried it into Jessica's room. She was still asleep. I sat down on the floor where I could see the doorway, and leaned my back against her crib. If whoever was prowling around upstairs decided to kidnap Jessica, I would spring up at him with my butcher knife.

I would probably get my picture in the newspaper. There would be a big headline: BABYSITTER THWARTS WOULD-BE KIDNAPPER. Of course, the headline might also read, INFANT DISAPPEARS; BABYSITTER FOUND DEAD. I shivered and clutched the knife tighter.

The footsteps stopped. I listened some more. My mouth felt dry and I had to keep changing the knife from one hand to the other so I could wipe my palms on my jeans. I waited but I heard nothing more for almost an hour. That hour seemed more like a week. Mrs. Athens had told me they would be home around ten o'clock and I counted the minutes. One-hundred-twenty-five more minutes until ten o'clock.

At nine-thirty, the footsteps started again. They went out of the room directly above me. I heard a door click shut. Then I heard water running. Probably the thief was washing off his fingerprints. No doubt he'd come downstairs any moment.

Mr. and Mrs. Athens got home right at ten. When I heard their car doors slam, I jumped up and ran to the kitchen and put the knife away. Mrs. Athens asked me if I'd had any trouble with Jessica and I said no, which was the truth.

As soon as Mrs. Athens paid me, I ran home and told Ma that there was someone in the Athens' house and that we should call the police.

"What do you mean?" she said. "Who's in their house?"

"I don't know who," I said. "Probably a burglar. All night long I heard footsteps walking around in the upstairs bedroom."

Ma said I probably just heard Grandpa Athens.

"Who?" I said.

She said, "Grandpa Athens. You know. Mr. Athens' father. He lives in the upstairs part of the house."

I stared at Ma. "You *knew* someone else was there?" I said. "Why didn't you tell me?"

"But you know Grandpa Athens lives there," Ma said. "He's always lived there, ever since they moved in."

I told her I didn't know that.

Ma looked at me as if I'd just said I didn't know what color my hair is. "How could you not know?" she said. "Of course you knew."

"I *didn't* know," I said, and I stomped off to bed. The truth is, I probably did know about Grandpa Athens, but I just never paid any attention. What difference does it make to a kid if there are two adults or three adults in the house across the street? It doesn't make any difference at all — unless you're asked to babysit.

#12

Class Pictures

Tomorrow I get my class picture taken. I can feel a huge pimple sprouting on my nose. Right there, on the end, where it will show the most.

It happens every year. No matter what day the class pictures are scheduled for, I get a big pimple on my nose or a huge, juicy cold sore on my mouth. One year I got a terrible sunburn the week before the class pictures were taken. My nose was peeling so much, I looked like I had leprosy.

The photographer said not to worry about it. He said the purpose of a class photograph is to capture me the way I really am at that point in time. I don't agree. To me, class photographs are not the time for realism. I don't want my true image captured for posterity. I don't want my future descendants to gaze at my picture someday and say, "Oh, look at that! Grandma had a big red pimple on her nose."

What I'd like is for every class picture to make me look beautiful. Of course, I know it won't happen. I am realistic enough to know that cameras do not lie. The trouble is, cameras *do* seem to exaggerate the truth, and never in my favor.

Every year I get my class picture taken. Every year when I see the result, I am horrified. My pictures never resemble me. My hair always looks either stringy or frizzed. My smile seems fake. The expression on my face looks like I just swallowed a piece of rotten fish. My class pictures are AWFUL. Every year. And the worst part of all is that every year my mother looks at the latest dreadful picture and says, "Oh, that's a good picture." My father agrees.

My sister always claims that the picture flatters me, no matter how terrible it really is. "Boy, did you luck out," she'll say. "Imagine getting a class picture that makes you look so much better than you do in person."

Her remarks don't bother me because I say the same thing about her class pictures. It does bother me, though, when my friends look at my picture and say it looks just like me. How can they say such a thing? I stare at the photograph, which bears only the most fleeting resemblance to me, and wonder how they can think it looks just like me. Is something wrong with their eyes? Are they being kind and trying to make me feel better about having such a rotten picture?

Last year, I showed my class picture to Karen, who is my best friend in the whole world, and begged her to tell me the truth. I said I wanted her honest, unbiased opinion of my picture. I held it in front of her and we both stared at it.

I saw an ugly distortion; my freckles were too dark and my teeth looked crooked and the overall effect was that of a girl who was sadly in need of plastic surgery on her nose. Karen looked at the very same photo, turned to me and said, "I love it. It's really you."

It will happen again this year; I know it will. I'll go in there tomorrow with a giant zit on the end of my nose and the photographer will immortalize it in all its flaming glory. Then my friends and family will declare that the resulting picture is the real me.

The trouble is, I suspect they're right.

#13

You Put *What* on Your Hair?

Last week in speech class, we gave demonstration speeches. Shirley demonstrated how to make no-bake cookies. She brought all the ingredients and the cooking utensils and she made the cookies while she talked. Then she passed them around so everyone got some. It was a great demonstration speech.

Andy demonstrated how to shine shoes. He had shoe polish and rags and even an electric buffer. He did a good job on the shoes but nobody in the class was too interested. Everyone wears tennis shoes or jogging shoes. Who wears shoes that have to be polished?

I wanted to give my demonstration on something of vital interest to everyone in the class. After much thought, I hit on the perfect topic. Hair. Everyone is interested in how their hair looks so I decided to give my demonstration speech on how to condition your hair so it is silky and shiny and has lots of bounce.

I'd read that if you put mayonnaise on your hair and then wrap your head with plastic wrap, it is a perfect conditioner. My plan was to demonstrate on myself. I would smear mayonnaise all over my head and work it into my hair. Then I would wrap plastic wrap around my hair, like a turban, and I'd keep that on while the next person gave his speech. Then I'd go in the bathroom, discard the plastic wrap and rinse all the mayonnaise out.

My teacher agreed to let me give my demonstration speech in two parts. Part one was smear and wrap; part two would be to let everyone see how shiny and bouncy my hair was after I rinsed out the mayonnaise.

Everything went fine during part one. Since one of the criteria for grading was to hold the attention of the audience, I was sure I had an A. The class laughed and hooted and urged me to use more mayonnaise. I had their undivided attention, there's no doubt of that. I dug my spoon into the jar and dropped big globs on my head. Then I massaged it into my hair. When my entire head resembled a bowl of egg salad, I wrapped the plastic wrap around and around, covering every inch of hair.

Amid spontaneous applause, I sat down to let the mayo do its job while I heard the next person's speech.

That's when the fire alarm went off. I couldn't believe it. We had not had a fire drill all year and now they were having one while my head was covered with mayonnaise and plastic wrap.

"Everyone line up. Quickly!" the teacher said.

I said I'd go rinse my hair and catch up with the class outside, but my teacher wouldn't hear of it. She said we had to get out of the building immediately because it might be a real fire. I tried to tell her that if it *was* a fire, I'd be perfectly safe with my head under the faucet, but she insisted that I line up and go outside with the rest of the class.

I've never been so humiliated in my life. I attracted more attention than the Fire Marshall who came to supervise our drill. Everyone who saw me burst out laughing and then yelled at someone else to look. Worst of all, the local TV station was short of news that day so they decided to film the fire drill. When the reporter saw me, she ran over, stuck a microphone in my face, and asked me my name.

When the fire drill finally ended and we were allowed to go back inside, I headed straight for the bathroom. That's when I discovered that mayonnaise doesn't rinse out. Not with cold water. Not with hot water. Not with hot water and a whole handful of the pink grainey soap that our school uses.

No matter how long I held my head in the sink, I couldn't get all of the mayonnaise out. I finally had to cut the rest of my classes and go home and get in the shower. Even then, it took nearly an hour and four different kinds of shampoo before I had nothing but hair on my head.

By then it was too late to go back to class and let everyone admire my shiny, bouncy hair. Instead of an A on my speech, I got an incomplete.

That night on the six o'clock news, there I was for all the world to see, looking like someone from outer space. And there was the reporter, cracking up right on camera as she said, "You put *what* on your hair?"

#14

Getting My First Bra

I wanted to wear a bra long before I needed one. When my friends began developing curves, I longed for my body to blossom, too. Instead, I remained straight as a board.

Faithfully, I did the exercises which were whispered from girl to girl, but they didn't help. When my worst enemy, Barbara, wore a bra to school, I jealously gritted my teeth. When my best friend, Judy, confided that her mother was taking her shopping to get a bra, I felt like crying.

It wasn't fair! Judy was three months younger than me. Why should she have curves when I did not? I wondered if there was something wrong with my hormones. What if my shape never changed? What if I became the first female to graduate from high school with the figure of a ten-year-old boy?

Each day I scrutinized my nude body in the mirror, hoping for some sign of impending womanhood. None was visible. Meanwhile, most of my friends began to resemble their mothers rather than their brothers. One day as I changed into my gym clothes, I realized I was the only girl in my gym class who still wore an undershirt instead of a bra. It was humiliating.

I decided to wear a bra, too, whether I needed one or not. There was just one problem: before I could get a bra, I had to tell my mother that I wanted one. Even though I wanted one desperately, it wasn't easy for me to talk about it.

I tried to hint; I said I was the only girl in my class who didn't wear a bra. Mom said not to worry about it. She said *she* had been slow to develop, too, and that my figure would arrive when the time was right for me. That was no help when I had to change clothes in gym class.

I don't know why I was embarrassed to ask Mom if I could have a bra. Maybe I was afraid she'd laugh at me. If I really needed one, I could have asked easily. Of course, if I needed one, Mom would have noticed and I wouldn't have to ask. At any rate, every time I got up my nerve to ask her, I chickened out.

Finally I decided to write her a note. But what if my brother found it and read it? I'd die right on the spot. I could just hear Mike blabbing to all his buddies how his flat-chested sister wanted a bra.

My solution was to write a tiny note and leave it somewhere that Mom would look but Mike would not.

I took a teeny piece of paper and printed in my tiniest handwriting: *Can I have a bra?* I put the note in my bed, way down between the sheets. Surely Mom would find it when she washed my sheets.

The next day, I rushed home from school and went straight to my room. I pulled back the bedspread to see if there might be fresh sheets on my bed. There weren't. I asked Mom when she planned to wash my sheets.

"I just changed the beds two days ago," she told me. "Did you spill something?"

I told her no. I was tempted to spill something, though, just to hurry things along.

I waited a couple of days and then I asked her again when she was going to wash my sheets. She gave me a funny look.

"What's the big concern with clean sheets all of a sudden?" she asked.

I shrugged and tried to look casual. "Oh, nothing," I said. "I was just wondering, that's all."

She told me if I wanted to strip my bed and wash the sheets I could go ahead and do it, but I said no, I would wait until she did the other beds.

She did them a few days later. When I got home from school, she told me right away that she'd washed my sheets. I held my breath. What if she hadn't found my note? It was so tiny, maybe she didn't notice it. Maybe she put it in the washing machine and it dissolved and went down the drain. Maybe I would wear little kids undershirts for the rest of my life.

"I found your note," she said. I waited. Was she going to laugh? Would she give me a lecture about not spending good money on something I don't need?

"If you want to go shopping tonight," Mom said, "we could buy you a bra then."

She smiled at me. She said we might as well go ahead and get two because I was sure to grow into them soon.

I wore my new bra the next day. It was lightly padded and I felt like a glamorous movie star.

When Judy saw me, she said, "I see you finally had to get a bra too. Aren't they awful?" She said she'd argued against getting one as long as she could, but her mother had insisted.

"I know what you mean," I said. "My mother made me get one too."

#15

In 100 Years, Who'll
Know the Difference?

My mother makes me furious. Whenever I'm upset about something, she always says, "In one hundred years, who'll know the difference?"

When she says that, she thinks it will calm me down. It never calms me down. It always makes me more upset. I hate having her tell me that whatever it is I'm so unhappy about really isn't important at all.

Once I tried out for my school's cheerleading squad. I spent weeks working on my audition routine and then, in the middle of the audition, my shoelace came untied and I tripped and fell, right in front of the judges. I didn't make the squad and when I got home, I cried and threw my shoes in the garbage can.

Mom said she was sorry I didn't make the cheering squad and she fixed my favorite dinner, which I couldn't eat, and then, when I was still carrying on at bedtime, she shrugged her shoulders and said, "In a hundred years, who'll know the difference?"

I got so angry, I refused to answer her.

Another time, on my birthday, I received a china tea set and as I lifted the little tea pot out of the package, it slipped out of my hand, fell to the floor and broke. I wept and refused to blow out the candles on my cake. Once again, Mom said those hated words: "In one hundred years, who'll know the difference?"

She said it so many times, in so many circumstances, that eventually she didn't have to say it at all. As soon as something bad happened that made me feel like screaming and crying, I found myself thinking: in one hundred years . . .

The year that I failed to make the cheering squad, I got the lead in the school play. If I had been on the cheering squad, I would not have tried out for the play, because play rehearsals and cheerleading practice were at the same time. Being in that play was the most exciting thing I've ever done.

When my aunt and uncle heard that I'd dropped the little tea pot they sent me, they not only sent a replacement, they sent a lovely hand-embroidered tablecloth to use at my tea parties. I don't play with tea sets anymore but I still have the tablecloth and I'll use it when I have a home of my own.

Still, it's hard to admit that Mom was right all these years, so I never told her how I feel. Last night I got my chance.

Mom's friend, Edna, came over and they decided to change their hair color. I don't know what went wrong. Maybe they got to talking and forgot the time and left the rinse on too long, or maybe there was something wrong with the package of hair color. Whatever happened, it was disasterville.

I got home at eleven o'clock and Mom was in the bathroom, crying. Her hair was green. Not just slightly green, like my hair gets if I swim in chlorinated pools all summer. This was bright, shamrock green. Maybe even glow-in-the-dark green.

I didn't blame her for crying and I wanted to say something that would make her feel better. I should have pointed out that she could wear a wig, but instead I said, "In one hundred years, who will know the difference?"

Mom just glared at me and poured more shampoo on her green hair.

#16

Double Trouble

It is truly miraculous that I am able to stand before you today, alive and healthy. No, I never had a horrible childhood disease. But I did have an ingenious gift for getting into trouble and when I think back on some of the things I did, it's a miracle that my parents didn't kill me before I reached my teens.

Usually I got into trouble with my friend, Emily, who lived next door. When we were together, we dreamed up things to do that neither of us would have done on our own. Our parents called us Double Trouble and often threatened to keep us apart.

My earliest memory is of myself and Emily, locked in the bathroom. Not by accident — by choice. The door was locked so that my babysitter could not come in and discover that Emily and I were creating a mural on the bathroom wall with my mother's lipstick and cold cream. The lipstick made line drawings; the cold cream worked for finger painting.

When my mother got home, she scolded us and sent Emily home, but she didn't yell and carry on the way she did when we cut our hair.

Emily used to have long, bouncy curls of the Shirley Temple variety. Her mother would roll her hair up in rollers every night, an ordeal which Emily hated. I had pigtails . . . thick, long braids that hung past my shoulders.

We cut the pigtails first. They were easy. Emily used my mother's sewing scissors, because they were the sharpest pair we could find. She had to hold the scissors with both hands in order to get enough pressure, and she cut those pigtails right off, while they were still braided.

Emily's curls were fun to cut, too. I did them one at a time, snipping as close to the scalp as I could so that the curls which fell to the floor were as long as possible.

Our plan was to glue the hair on my baby sister, who was nearly a year old and still completely bald. We couldn't agree on whether to give her Emily's curls or my pigtails, so we decided to do one side of her head one way and the other side the other way. We found some glue in my father's desk, smeared it on half of Sophie's bald head and stuck Emily's curls into the glue. The curls didn't hold together as well as we had hoped so we added more glue. It was hard to keep the hair from sticking to our fingers and we had to keep wiping our hands on our clothes.

When we tried to glue a pigtail on the other side of Sophie's head, it wouldn't stick at all. It was too heavy. We decided we should unbraid it, glue the individual parts on, and then braid it again after the glue was dry.

We never did find out if that plan would work or not. Sophie got tired of sitting still and started to howl. Mother came to see what was wrong, took one look, and howled louder than Sophie. Emily ran home, leaving me to explain by myself, but she was soon back with her tearful mother, who accused me of being a troublemaker and said Emily could not play with me anymore.

This made my mother angry. She quit yelling at me and informed Emily's mother that I was never naughty when I was alone, only when I was with Emily. She suggested that Emily was the troublemaker and I was hardly more than an innocent bystander.

Our mothers soon calmed down and apologized for losing their tempers with each other. They agreed that Emily and I required closer supervision when we were together and for the rest of that summer they watched us like private detectives.

It wasn't any fun at all.

#17

How I Quit Biting My Fingernails

I can't remember a time when I didn't bite my fingernails. Instead of sucking my thumb like most babies do, I'd lay in my crib and bite my fingernails.

It used to drive my mother nuts. She was always ordering me to quit biting my fingernails. She nagged and pleaded and threatened. She didn't understand that I never did it on purpose. Usually, I didn't even know I was doing it until she'd tell me to stop.

I never could understand why it bothered her so much. It isn't as if it's illegal or pornographic. I would have to trim my fingernails anyway — everyone does — so what's the difference whether I used fingernail scissors or my teeth?

I admit my nails never looked too good when I bit them, but it wasn't actually harmful, like smoking. Nobody ever got cancer and died because they bit their fingernails.

I never ate the fingernails. I tried swallowing them once, but they scratched my throat, so after that I just bit them off and spit them out.

Once, when I was three years old, my mother showed me a photograph of the statue, Venus de Milo. She's the one whose arms are broken off above the elbow. As I stared at the unfortunate woman with no arms, Mom implied that's what happens to people who bite their fingernails. She suggested that unless I quit biting my fingernails immediately, I, too, would end up without arms.

Even at the age of three, I didn't buy that story. Biting my fingernails didn't hurt. The only pain involved was the pain of listening to my mother yell at me. But I knew that if I chomped off a whole finger and then nibbled my way up my arm, it would hurt plenty and I wasn't about to try it.

When I started kindergarten, Mom discussed the problem with my teacher. The teacher said I probably bit my fingernails because I was nervous and Mom assured her there was nothing for me to be nervous about. Secretly, I knew I was nervous because I was afraid of getting yelled at for biting my fingernails, but I didn't say that.

By the time I was in first grade, I decided that biting my fingernails was best done in private. If Mom didn't catch me doing it, she couldn't yell at me.

She always knew though. She could tell from how my nails looked that I had chewed them off. She bought some bitter tasting liquid and painted my fingernails with it. It tasted terrible and took all the fun out of biting my nails. But I continued to bite them anyway. Partly it was habit. And partly I was stubborn. I figured they were my fingernails and I should have a right to do anything I wanted to with them, as long as it didn't hurt anybody else.

This year, I quit. Cold turkey. One day it was nibble, munch, and the next day, nothing. I quit because my mother finally came up with a good reason why I should stop.

Money.

She bribed me to quit by promising me the new ten-speed bike I wanted. If I would go six months without biting my fingernails, the bike was mine.

It wasn't hard once I made up my mind. Now I have the bike, and I also have nails that look nice. It's wonderful to have fingernails with white on the end rather than jagged nubs. For the first time in my life, I don't keep my hands in my lap when I am with other people. I no longer curl my fingers into fists so that my friends won't notice my stubby fingernails.

I wish I'd quit biting my nails years ago. I don't dare tell Mom that though. She'd really yell at me then.

#18

Garbage Gifts

I used to get "garbage gifts" from my Aunt Marie. My parents said it was rude to call them that, but I couldn't think of a better way to describe them. Garbage gifts are presents that you know, from the minute you open them, you will never, ever use. When you get a garbage gift, you want to throw it in the trash can.

I never actually threw my garbage gifts away. I put them in the Goodwill box, just in case someone, somewhere might want them.

Almost everyone has at least one source of garbage gifts. For most kids, it's an older relative, someone who doesn't see you for years at a time and has no idea how old you are or what kinds of things you like to do.

Aunt Marie is really my great aunt, and she hasn't seen me since I was six months old. Apparently she didn't realize how much time has passed since then. One year for my birthday, Aunt Marie sent me sing-along tapes of nursery rhymes.

(Sings in fake small-child voice:)
"Twinkle, twinkle, little star . . ."
According to the box, the sing-along tapes were appropriate for ages three to five. I was in junior high.

Another time, she sent me mittens with cutesy kittens embroidered on them. I always opened Aunt Marie's present first, to get it over with.

My parents said it was the thought that counted. They made me write thank-you notes to Aunt Marie and pretend to like the sing-along tapes and the cutesy kitty mittens. I made my notes as brief as possible.

Last year, I thought I had figured out a way to educate Aunt Marie so she wouldn't keep wasting her money on gifts I'll never use. I bought a present for her, wrapped it, and had it ready to add to the box that Mom always sends to Aunt Marie for her birthday. I figured when Aunt Marie opened my present, it would make her think twice before she sent me something inappropriate.

When Mom started packing the box for Aunt Marie, she picked up my present, felt of it, and said, "It feels like a ping-pong paddle."

I said that's exactly what it was. Mom told me Aunt Marie is sixty-nine years old and will have no use for a ping-pong paddle. I said I didn't expect her to use it.

And that's when Mom told me about Aunt Marie's life. Aunt Marie lost her husband when she was thirty years old; he died in a fire which also gutted their home. Her only child, a son, was killed ten years later, in the war. Aunt Marie doesn't have much money and she probably goes without something she needs herself in order to remember all of us with gifts on our birthdays and at Christmas. She does it because we are the only family she has left.

"I know the things she sends you are too babyish," Mom said, "but she sends them out of love. And if you want to send something to Aunt Marie, it must be chosen with love, too."

I wondered what it would be like to have your only family be people you never see.

I returned the ping-pong paddle to the store and got a refund. With the money, I bought Aunt Marie one of those fancy little baskets filled with dried apricots and raspberry jam and tea biscuits from England. I wrote her a letter, too, and tucked it in the basket. I told her what grade I'm in and that I like to read mysteries and play tennis. I enclosed one of my class pictures.

Aunt Marie sent me a thank you letter and said she was surprised to see what a lovely young lady I was. She told me dried apricots are her favorite treat.

On my birthday that year, I opened Aunt Marie's gift first, as usual. It was a dozen new tennis balls, good ones.

I've never had another garbage gift from Aunt Marie.

Part Two:

MONOLOGS
FOR
BOYS

#19

The School Yard Bully

Andrew Buckingham is a bully. He's mean to younger kids, and once, when Andrew thought nobody was around, Clancy Schuman saw Andrew kick a little dog. He said when the dog yelped, Andrew laughed, and kicked it again.

If there's anything in this world I can't stand, it's a bully. I never did like Andrew Buckingham and after I heard about the dog, I just plain detested him.

The problem with bullies is that it's hard to know what to do about them. Most bullies pick out one kid at a time for their victim. Usually, it's a kid who is small for his age or who is somehow different than the other kids. Then the bully hassles that one kid mercilessly.

That's what Andrew did to Clancy. I don't know if it was because Andrew found out that Clancy saw him kick the dog and blabbed it all over school, or whether he was already picking on Clancy when the dog incident happened.

Day after day, Andrew would go up to Clancy on the school yard and insult him. If Clancy talked back, Andrew punched him. If Clancy ignored the insults, Andrew called him a chicken. Either way, Clancy couldn't win. It got so he made up excuses not to go out during recess because he knew Andrew would be waiting for him the minute he left the building.

The rest of us watched these proceedings nervously. We felt sorry for Clancy, but we also knew that anyone who intervened would be the next victim. Nobody was eager to claim that honor.

Why didn't Clancy tell the teacher? I guess Clancy thought it was better to get punched around by Andrew than to be known as a tattle-tale. In our school, tattling was a sin even worse than bullying.

And then one day, Clancy fought back. I don't know why that

particular day was any different than all the days before, but during afternoon recess, Clancy was shooting baskets when Andrew went over to him and announced that *he* wanted to shoot baskets. Clancy went on dribbling the ball.

"Didn't you hear me, Turkey?" Andrew said. "I said, it's *my* turn, so hand over the basketball."

The minute Andrew raised his voice, a crowd gathered. We all stood in a semi-circle around the side of the basketball court, waiting to see what would happen.

Clancy dribbled again, lifted his arms and aimed the ball for the basket. It hit the rim and bounced away. Andrew lunged for it, but Clancy was too quick for him. He darted forward, tipped the ball away from Andrew, caught it and dribbled back to the free-throw line.

Andrew got red in the face. He swore at Clancy and said he wanted the basketball NOW.

Clancy shook his head. Andrew started toward him, his fists clenched, but Clancy stood his ground, clutching that basketball tight to his chest.

As soon as Andrew was close enough, he socked Clancy's shoulder. Clancy winced but he didn't let go of the ball. Andrew whacked him again.

My heart was pounding. I didn't want Clancy to give in — but I didn't want to watch him get beat up, either.

After Andrew punched him the second time, Clancy set the basketball on the ground next to his feet. Then, without saying a word, he swung his fist at Andrew. Andrew ducked — and Clancy missed him.

Andrew's next blow caught Clancy on the cheek — and sent him staggering backwards, away from the basketball. Andrew leaned forward to pick it up.

That's when I looked around. There were two dozen of us watching and I felt ashamed that none of us would help Clancy. I wasn't eager to have Andrew punch me out, but I knew I couldn't stand there and watch any longer.

As Andrew bent to pick up the basketball, I stepped forward and kicked it out of his reach. I kicked it toward Clancy and if I live to be a thousand, I'll never forget the gratitude in Clancy's eyes as he looked to see who had kicked that ball to him.

I didn't have long to enjoy the look, because Andrew started toward me, and I could practically see the smoke pouring out of his ears.

"So, you want in the game, do you, Twerp?" he growled.

I stood next to Clancy, my knees shaking. "Clancy had the ball," I said. "You have no right to take it away from him."

I braced myself for the blows that I was sure were coming. And then something extraordinary happened. Two other kids stepped forward, one on either side of me, and they told Andrew I was right; that it was Clancy's ball.

As soon as they did that, the rest of the kids surged forward. They gathered around Clancy and me and they *all* told Andrew to bug off and leave Clancy alone. It was no longer Andrew against Clancy; it was Andrew against the whole fifth grade class.

Just then, the bell rang. Recess was over and we had to go back inside. It was a relief to sit at my desk. I had been certain I was going to be punched to a pulp and left to die on the basketball court.

Our collective triumph over Andrew exhilarated me but I kept wondering why we didn't stand up to him sooner. If all of us had stepped in to defend Clancy the first time Andrew picked on him, the whole sorry situation would never have happened. All it took was one show of unity to stop a bully; so why didn't one of us ever suggest to the others that we do it? Why did we let Andrew pick on Clancy all those months?

I have no answers. I can only say that I'm glad we finally put a stop to it. Recess is a lot more fun now.

#20

Will I Have to Get a Shot?

I learned recently that different people have different levels of pain. This information is a great relief to me. All this time, I've thought I was just chicken; now it turns out that maybe some things hurt me more than they hurt other people. Things like getting vaccinated or having a shot of Novocain at the dentist.

"This shouldn't hurt at all," my dentist says, but I know I must grip the arms of the chair and curl my toes tightly into my shoes to prevent myself from jumping up and rushing out of his office, still wearing the little paper bib.

When I was small and learned I was going to the doctor, I only wanted to know one thing: Do I have to get a shot?

My mother did not want to lie to me, but she didn't want me to be hysterical with fear before we even left home, either. Her answer always began with, "Yes, but."

"Yes, but it's just a teensy tiny little needle; you won't even feel it." Or, "Yes, but it will be over before you know it and on the way home we'll stop for ice cream."

I never heard the part about *teensy tiny* or *ice cream*. The second she got to, "Yes, but," I started to cry and any further attempt at conversation was futile.

Our family doctor decided that my fear was caused by ignorance and he set out to instruct me on every facet of medicine which he thought I was old enough to understand. He explained how antibiotics work. He gave me a color drawing of a person, with all the muscles showing.

He even confided to my parents that he hoped I would be so interested in his explanations that I would consider a career in medicine. Each time I saw Dr. Deal, he asked me what I wanted to be when I grew up.

His hopes were dashed the day my sister fell while she was

carrying a glass of lemonade. The glass broke and Betsy got a nasty gash on her arm. We rushed to Dr. Deal's office, with Betsy shrieking, and Mom looking pale. I stared at the blood which seeped through the dish towel that Betsy held on the wound and asked, "Will she have to get a shot?" Betsy shrieked louder.

She not only needed a tetanus shot, she also needed a few stitches and Dr. Deal suggested that I be allowed to stay and watch. Betsy didn't object, so I stood beside her and watched as Dr. Deal got out antiseptic and cotton swabs and a tiny, thin needle. He picked up what he called special thread, made just for little girls who cut their arms, and threaded the needle with it. As he worked, he explained what he was doing and he used words that even Betsy could understand.

I did OK while he applied the antiseptic but the minute he picked up that needle, my stomach began doing cartwheels. From that point on, Dr. Deal might just as well have spoken Chinese, for all I understood. I swallowed hard. I tried to steady myself by putting my hand on the table where Betsy lay.

When he stuck the needle into Betsy's arm, I bolted out of the office. I was afraid I was going to vomit all over Dr. Deal's waiting room, but I managed to hold it until I got outside. Then I crawled into the car and lay trembling on the back seat. My hands felt clammy and there were beads of sweat on my forehead.

When Mom and Betsy came out to the car, Betsy complained because I got to lie down on the seat and not wear my seat belt while she had to sit up in front. She pointed out that *she* was the one who had cut her arm and had to get stitches. But Mom looked at me and said I should stay right where I was.

After that, Dr. Deal quit giving me diagrams and stopped explaining everything he did. He never again asked me what I wanted to be when I grew up.

I'm much older now and when I need medical treatment, I'm able to understand why. Yet, I still get knots in my stomach if I know I'm scheduled for a check-up. And my first thought is always the same: will I have to get a shot?

#21

The World's Longest Monopoly Game

When I was eight years old, my dad taught me how to play Monopoly. Our game lasted more than three years. Instead of ending the game when I went bankrupt, Dad made me a loan. He explained how banks make loans and how interest is charged and we worked it all out on paper. Then I kept playing on borrowed money.

We continued the game the next day. Whenever we had time, we played Monopoly and I did so well with my borrowed money that a few days later, *he* went bankrupt and I had to make him a loan.

We kept going back and forth, with first one of us winning and then the other, but we never ended the game.

Eventually, our loan papers got pretty complicated and so we made a big chart. We labeled it *The World's Longest Monopoly Game,* and we kept track of all our debits and credits on the chart. Since we always played Monopoly at the kitchen table, we hung the chart on the refrigerator, where we could refer to it easily.

My friends used to look at it when they came over. Everyone thought it was neat that my dad and I had the world's longest Monopoly game. It was something no other kid had and it made me feel special.

The divorce happened when I was eleven. Dad and I didn't play Monopoly as much that year because he was gone a lot. When he was home, he and Mom argued all the time and I didn't like to hear it, so I spent most of my time over at Eddie's house.

One night when I came home from Eddie's, Dad was gone. Three weeks later he moved to Los Angeles. He took a new job and rented a house. I missed him a lot. Everything had happened so fast and I never understood why. I took the Monopoly chart off the refrigerator but I didn't throw it away. I rolled it up and stored it in the back of my closet, just in case Dad ever changed his mind and came back home. This may sound crazy, but it was almost like my chart from the world's longest Monopoly game was proof that my dad still loved me, even though he didn't live with me anymore.

The next summer, Dad sent money for me to come and visit him. I could hardly wait. All I thought about was how great it was going to be to see him again and how much fun we would have. I had so many things to tell him about school.

I packed the Monopoly game and the chart in my suitcase. They took up quite a bit of space, but I knew it would be worth it. I thought we could put the chart on Dad's refrigerator and start the game again, right where we'd left off.

On the way from the airport to his house, Dad told me there was someone he wanted me to meet. Her name was Ellen and he said he planned to marry her. Ellen had a son, Frankie, who was a year younger than I.

Ellen was OK, but Frankie was a nerd. He bragged all the time and tried to impress me. What really got me, though, was that he called Dad, "Dad." The first time I heard him do it, I wanted to punch him in the mouth. This was *my* dad. Not his. To make it even worse, Dad liked it that Frankie called him, "Dad." I could tell by the way he smiled and looked at Ellen.

When I unpacked my things, I didn't show Dad the Monopoly chart. I left it in my suitcase. I was saving it for a surprise, for a night when Ellen and Frankie weren't with us.

The four of us went to Disneyland.

The four of us went to Knotts Berry Farm.

The four of us took a tour of a movie studio. Everything was fun, but I kept wishing I could spend a day alone with Dad, just the two of us. I'd been so lonely for him, since the divorce. I missed talking to him and watching Monday Night Football together and playing our special game. In his letters, he always said he missed me too.

One morning, Dad said we were going to have dinner that night at Ellen's house. Until then, she and Frankie had come to Dad's house or else we met them somewhere.

I was kind of curious to see where Ellen and Frankie lived. It was an ordinary house, but it had one thing I didn't expect.

I saw it as soon as I went out to the kitchen. It hung on Frankie's refrigerator: a big chart that said, *The World's Longest Monopoly Game.*

I looked at it for a long time — the loans, the interest rates, the pay-offs. All those months when I was home, thinking of Dad and missing him and wishing he'd come back, he was here, playing Monopoly with Frankie.

Why did he have to play *our* game with Frankie? Didn't he know how special it was?

I stayed with Dad another week, but I never unpacked my Monopoly chart. I knew that even if Dad and I had time alone to play, it wouldn't be the same. It would never be the same again.

When I got home, I put the chart back in my closet. I'm no longer the only kid in the world who has one, but I'll keep it forever, anyway.

#22

If It's OK With Mom,
Is It OK With You?

The summer was nearly over. Jason and I were bored and broke when we saw the ad. *Help wanted. One day only. Set up traveling carnival and earn BIG MONEY.*

"Let's do it," Jason said.

I looked at him, to see if he was serious. He was.

I knew exactly what my parents would say if I asked permission to work at a traveling carnival. My mother would say, "Absolutely not. Those carnival workers are nothing but riff-raff and I don't want you associating with them." My father would say, "Sorry, pal. I admire your initiative in trying to earn money, but you'd better stick to lawn mowing for awhile."

When I told Jason this, he snorted with disgust. "Lawn mowing. In one day as a carnival worker, you will earn as much as you'd get in a week mowing lawns. And it will be a lot more exciting. This," he declared, "will be a day you'll never forget."

Then he told me that instead of asking our parents for permission, we were going to finagle.

The first step in finagling was to decide which of our parents might be the most likely to give in and say *yes*. We decided on my mom. Jason instructed me to wait until Mom was concentrating on something else before I spoke. I caught her when she was reading a recipe and trying to measure the ingredients, which turned out to be a good time. I said, "Mom, I have a chance to earn some money tomorrow. Jason's going to do it and he wants me to go with him. If it's OK with Dad, is it OK with you?"

Mom squinted at her cookbook and said, "Well, I suppose if your father thinks it's all right, you can go."

Next Jason said to approach my father but to wait until he was thinking about something else. Ideal times, according to

Jason, are when he's watching a ball game on TV or reading his favorite section of the newspaper. I caught Dad when he was talking back to a broadcaster on TV.

I said, "Mom says I can go with Jason tomorrow to work at the carnival. Is that OK with you, too?"

He nodded and said, "All right," and kept right on arguing with the man on TV.

Next stop was Jason's house. It was a breeze, just like he said it would be. All he had to do was say that I had already spoken with my parents and they both agreed that working at the carnival was a fine idea.

I was impressed. Jason said it was common sense. He said even the most conscientious parents would rather not have to ask a billion questions about when you're going and who's taking you and who else will be there and what time will you be home. If they think some other parent has already gone through all of that, they're happy to accept the other parent's judgment.

He said finagling with parents can work over and over again, so long as nobody finds out how you're doing it. He also said finagling should be used only for events which are critical to my happiness and not wasted on unimportant things like eating chocolate chip cookies before dinner.

He warned me that the less said about our day at the carnival, the better. He said we would pocket our wages and keep quiet. Otherwise, we could stir up a hornet's nest of trouble.

I said it was going to be hard to finally do something interesting and then not tell anyone about it.

Jason said, "If you go home and flash two twenty dollar bills and tell how two scumballs tried to get you to spend it on marijuana, your parents are immediately going to insist that they never gave you permission to work at any carnival. They might even call my parents and get me in a pickle, too. Worst of all, they'll question each other about exactly what was said and then they'll put two and two together and come up with the fact that you finagled them into giving permission. And then there *will* be some excitement in your life."

I agreed it would be best to keep my mouth shut.

I never worked so hard as I did at the carnival. By the end of the afternoon, every muscle in my body ached. The man in charge swore at me when I had to go to the bathroom while we were driving in the stakes for the biggest tent, and the pay wasn't as great as we had thought it would be, either. We earned a little more than we would have if we had mowed lawns all day, but not much more. I sure didn't have to worry about flashing any twenties around.

I dragged myself home and took a bath without being told. As I soaked my aching muscles, I decided it was the most miserable day I'd ever spent. I would have fallen asleep there in the tub, except I was afraid I might drown.

When I went down to dinner, my parents were waiting for me. My father held the evening newspaper. My mother's eyes were flashing fire. There, on page four, was a story about the carnival — and a picture of some workers driving tent stakes into the ground. I don't need to tell you who one of those workers was.

I was grounded for a week and I had to donate my meager earnings to a charity. My mother called Jason's mother and told her how we had finagled them and he got grounded, too. Jason got to keep his money, which didn't seem fair, but I knew better than to argue.

Jason was right about one thing: it was a day I'll never forget. I worked too hard for a mean boss, made very little money, and felt guilty because I'd tricked my folks. At the end, I was still bored and broke, only now I was grounded, too.

I am never going to finagle again. It isn't worth it.

#23

What Mother Doesn't Know Won't Hurt Me

Mothers should not be told certain things. I don't mean that kids should lie or be intentionally sneaky. I just mean there are times when it's only smart to keep your mouth shut.

For example, I'm quite certain I did the right thing when I failed to mention to my mother that I went tobogganing with the cast on my leg. It doesn't snow often where I live, but when it does, there's a fine hill at the end of our block where all the kids bring sleds and inner tubes and toboggans.

It snowed while my broken leg was still in the cast, which hardly seemed fair. It was bad enough to miss out on the entire basketball season, but to miss what might be the only snowstorm of the year was just too much.

When my friend, Jeff, stopped by to say hello and to tell me he and the gang were taking his toboggan down to the hill, I couldn't stand it. I got a plastic bag — the kind that is used to line garbage cans — and put it over my cast and tied it tight with string. I got my jacket and a pair of mittens and my crutches and off I went.

I had to sit at the back of the toboggan with my legs straight out in front of me. I sat on my crutches so they wouldn't fall off. It was hard on my rear end, but it was the only way I could think of to take the crutches with me, since I needed both hands to hold on to the toboggan.

It was impossible to steer, but Jeff aimed me down the hill and gave me a shove. I flew down that hill, bumping and bouncing and clinging to the toboggan. It was great! I couldn't wait to do it again.

It was hard to climb back up the hill because the tips of the crutches sank too far into the snow. I struggled on, though. The ride down was worth the effort. I made it five times. On the last ride, either Jeff didn't aim me straight or else the toboggan hit a snow-covered rock because I veered too far to the left and crashed into a row of juniper bushes.

The crash jarred my leg, which scared me. By then, I was too tired to make it up the hill again anyway, so I headed for home.

When I got there, I threw what was left of the plastic bag away, put my wet mittens in the back of my closet to dry, and lay down on my bed. That's where I was when my mother got home.

She said she thought I looked a little pale, and I said I was just tired, and she said anyone would be tired, having to walk around school all day on crutches. Then she offered to bake my favorite chocolate cake, the kind with four layers and butter cream frosting that I usually get only on my birthday. She said it would be a special treat because I had to stay inside with my broken leg when she knew I would rather be out in the snow, playing with my friends.

I said, "thank you," but that's all I said. I would have been crazy to mention anything about a toboggan.

#24

Weird Richard

One of my best friends is weird. His name is Richard and he is always called Richard, never Ricky or Dick. Richard is wimpy looking. It isn't just that he's short. It's more that he looks like it would take a major miracle for him to catch a baseball.

Richard has no interest in catching baseballs or any other kind of balls. He does not like sports, rock music or automobiles. He prefers water to soft drinks and wishes McDonald's would offer steamed broccoli instead of french fries.

I got to be friends with Richard when my family rented the house next door to his. We moved in at the end of June so I wasn't in school, and there wasn't any place to make new friends except right in my own neighborhood. Richard is the only kid my age within four blocks.

Richard has his own computer and I asked him to teach me how to run it. We started playing computer games and I have to admit, Richard's good. He may be a wimp, but he's a smart wimp. He even invented some new games and programmed the computer to do them. We had a good time that first summer, playing the computer games.

After we'd known each other a few weeks, I asked Richard if he wanted to call up strangers on the telephone. He asked me why I would want to talk to someone I don't know, and I said I thought all kids did that when they're bored. I explained how most kids call somebody up and ask a dumb question like, "Is your refrigerator running?" and then, when the person says, "Yes," the kid says, "Go out and catch it."

Richard said that was stupid and I agreed.

I told him how my friends and I, in my old town, used to call people up and say we were from the Lottery Commission and the person had just won $1,000 a week for twenty years. Hardly anyone ever hung up on us. Usually, they got excited and asked what they had to do to get the money, and then we'd say, "Go get a job," and hang up.

I thought it was hilarious, but when I told Richard about it, he said what if we called a person who truly was poor, someone who had no money and was trying hard to find a job. He said it wouldn't be funny then; it would be cruel. After Richard said that, I never called up strangers anymore. My parents would kill me if they knew I ever did it at all.

When school started that fall, Richard and I walked together. It was nice not to have to walk to a new school alone. Gradually, I made other friends. Richard had no other friends. He's the kind of kid that other kids make fun of, because they don't understand him.

Richard gets all A's in school, but when it comes to getting along with a group of kids, he's practically incompetent. He probably would never have made friends with me except there I was, right next door, where it was impossible to avoid me. And since I didn't know anyone else in town, I made the effort to get to know Richard. No one else was willing to do that.

At first we walked to school together and walked home together, but then I joined the track team which practices after school, so Richard had to walk home alone. I told him to join the team too, but he didn't want to.

I made several friends, including Mark, who will probably be my friend forever, or at least until we finish high school. Mark asked me one time why I hang around with Richard when Richard is so weird. I said I like Richard, and Mark said I was the only person in the world who did.

Sometimes I think he's right. The strange thing is, Richard never asked why I hang around with Mark. He seems to know why, even though I was friends with him first.

Once I invited Richard to come over when Mark was there. I thought if they had a chance to get acquainted, they might like each other, but as soon as Richard got there and found out it wasn't just the two of us, he made up some excuse why he had to leave. Mark said it was proof that Richard is weird and we were better off without him.

My dad says Richard isn't weird, he's just a loner and loners often grow up to be scientists or symphony conductors or famous artists. He said Richard will probably discover the cure for cancer, or invent a new kind of computer that revolutionizes American business. Dad said when I'm forty years old and come back to my class reunion, everyone will be hoping that Richard shows up so they can say they saw their old friend, Richard, again. He says some day even Mark will be pretending that he and Richard were best buddies while they were growing up.

I don't think Richard will come to any class reunions, whether he's famous or not. But I hope Dad's right about him because even though Richard is weird, he's still my friend.

#25

Thoughts on a First Date

That was the worst movie I ever saw. What a jerk I am! How could I take Sharon to such a rotten film on our first date? First and only date. She'll never go out with me again. She probably thinks I always go to movies like that.

She hated it. I know she did. She hated the movie and now she hates me too, for suggesting it. Tomorrow, when she tells her friends about this, she'll probably call me Killer, the guy who loves blood and gore. She'll warn them to stay away from me. "Stay away from Killer," she'll say. "He's bad news." I'll probably never get another date with anyone.

I should have asked her if she wanted to leave. She probably wanted to walk out. That's why she went to the restroom so often. It wasn't because she needed to go to the bathroom, it was because she couldn't stand to watch the movie. Why didn't I catch on? I should have realized that nobody goes to the restroom four times in one hour unless they have a kidney problem. I should have known she wanted to leave.

But what if she liked the movie? I'd really look like a jerk then, if I suggested leaving right in the middle of a movie that she loves. Next time I ask a girl to go to a movie it's going to be something by Walt Disney. You can't go wrong with Walt Disney.

I wonder if she wants to get something to eat before we go home? Probably not. She probably wants to go straight home, by the fastest route possible. Who would blame her? The sooner she gets away from Killer, the better.

On the other hand, maybe she's hungry. Maybe she's starving to death. Maybe she was too nervous to eat dinner, just like I was. If I take her home without getting anything to eat, she'll not only think I'm a jerk, she'll think I'm a stingy jerk. Killer, the stingy jerk. He loves blood and gore, but he's too tight to spring for a burger and fries.

I wonder if she would let me kiss her goodnight. I don't know how to kiss a girl goodnight. It always looks easy on TV, but those guys get to rehearse.

I'll only get one shot at it. What if I mess up? What if I knock her glasses off? What do we do about our noses, to keep them from bumping? And where do I put my hands? Do I put them on her shoulders or just let them dangle by my sides? Killer, the stingy jerk who doesn't know how to kiss.

What if she slaps me? What if I try to kiss her goodnight and she slaps me? Maybe I should shake her hand instead.

She'll probably laugh if I ask her to go out with me again. Maybe I should wait and call her up. It'll be easier to have her say *no* on the telephone than to hear her laugh at me in person.

Guys probably call her up all the time. Older guys. The ones that know how to pick a decent movie. The ones that know how to kiss. She can go out with anybody she wants. Why would she choose Killer the Jerk?

She says she had a good time tonight, but she's probably just being polite. She doesn't want to hurt my feelings.

Well, here goes. I'm going to ask her if she wants to go out with me again next Saturday. I wonder if there are any good Walt Disney movies in town. *Snow White* would be nice. Or *Dumbo*. Everybody loves *Dumbo*.

On the other hand, she might think *Dumbo* is too babyish. She'd think I was a real jerk, taking her to a kiddie movie.

I know what I'll do. If she says yes, I'll ask *her* to choose the movie this time. That's what I'll do. I don't care if it's *Dumbo* or *Rambo* as long as I don't have to decide.

(Pause one beat.) She said YES! I can't believe it! She wants to go out with me again next Saturday. Maybe I'm not such a jerk after all.

#26

Hero, Turkey, Friend: That's My Dad

When I was small, I thought my dad could do anything in the world. I believed he was the strongest man alive and the smartest and the richest.

I had good reason for these beliefs. He must be the strongest; he could lift me up over his head, couldn't he? He could open the most stubborn jar of peanut butter in one twist and he split logs with an axe so heavy that I couldn't even pick it up.

As for smart, my dad knew everything. He answered questions about where the clouds go at night and where the sun is on a rainy day. He knew why mother cats have kittens instead of puppies, and which tracks in the woods were deer and which were raccoons. He even knew how to fix broken tricycles.

If my dad ever worried about how he was going to pay the electric bill, I didn't know it. I knew only that when we went grocery shopping, Dad always had a quarter in his pocket for the horsey ride. Always. Sometimes, I didn't even have to ask. I would just look at Dad and he would grin at me and I knew that meant I could climb up on the black and white horse and he would drop a quarter in the slot to start the motor.

While I rode the horse, I was a cowboy herding cattle or the sheriff chasing a bank robber. I was a prince, riding full speed to rescue a child from danger. I could feel the wind in my face, and hear the applause of the onlookers.

By the time I outgrew the horsey ride, I realized that Dad didn't know everything. It was a shock. The first time I needed help with a homework assignment and Dad didn't know the answer, I was stunned. He took me to the library and we looked up the answer together. Still, I felt sad; my teacher knew the capital of Ireland, but until we looked it up, Dad didn't.

He must have sensed my disenchantment because on the way home, he told me that no person in the world can know everything. The key to knowledge, he said, is to know where to go to find the information you need. He said knowing how to use a library was one of the most important skills I could acquire.

At the time, I thought he was just making an excuse because he had not known the capital of Ireland.

When I realized that maybe Dad wasn't the smartest person in the world after all, I also began to suspect that he wasn't the strongest. As we watched a football game on TV one Monday night, I asked him why he never played football. He said he tried out for football his first year of high school, but he didn't make the team and he never tried out again. He said so much aggressive physical contact wasn't his style; he prefers golf or swimming.

I could accept that he liked golf and swimming better than playing football. But it was hard to accept that he didn't make the team.

So he wasn't the strongest man, after all, and he wasn't the smartest. It didn't take long to learn that he also wasn't the richest. When Stevie Lower, who lived next door, got a European racing bike for his eighth birthday, I immediately launched a campaign to get a European racing bike for *my* birthday. I soon learned that quarters for a horsey ride were one thing; nine-hundred-dollar bikes were something else again.

"We can't afford it," Dad told me. Plain and simple. "We can't afford it." While I was digesting that astounding piece of news, he added, "And even if I could afford it, I wouldn't buy it for you because no eight-year-old kid in the world needs a bike like that."

I cried. I pleaded. I begged him to take out a loan. But there was no arguing with the man. He told me he was sorry, but the matter was settled and there would be no further discussion.

That's when I decided he might not be the strongest, smartest or richest father in the world, but he was quite definitely the meanest.

The hero was gone. The ogre had arrived. I began to notice things about my dad that I didn't like. Funny how he acquired so many bad habits all of a sudden. Things like wearing his hair too long in back when the current style was for short cuts. And the way he talked to strangers! We'd be standing in line at the grocery store and instead of paging through the magazines on the rack or staring out the window, Dad would talk to the person behind us in the line. First thing you know, they'd be trading opinions on who would win the American League pennant this year, or whether the President would veto something that Congress had passed.

It was embarrassing. It got so I didn't like to be seen in public with him.

As I grew older, my feelings for my father changed one more time. Now I know that Dad let me ride the horsey so I would imagine myself accomplishing wonderful things. He answered my questions and took me to the library so I could learn how to achieve my imaginings.

He refused to waste money on something I didn't need so that I would value the important things in life and not covet the unimportant. He talked to strangers — and I gradually became aware that I can learn something from every person I meet. He found pleasure in the sports he played well — and appreciated someone else's talent for football. From watching him, I saw it was fun to participate and also fun to cheer from the stands.

Dad started as my hero, was demoted to the role of turkey, and gradually became my friend. You might even say we've come full circle because, in some ways, he's still my hero. And he always will be.

#27

Come to Church Camp; Learn to Kiss

When I was twelve, my parents sent me to a summer camp that was sponsored by a church. They said the camp would teach me religious basics and help me appreciate the beauties of nature.

They were right. The only boring part was the daily class in religion, but even that wasn't too bad because instead of listening to the instructor, everyone wrote long notes to each other. Unlike regular school, there was no test at the end of the week, so it didn't matter if we paid attention or not.

It was at church camp that I learned to kiss. Before arriving at camp, I had thought a great deal about kissing. I even practiced once, with a mirror. I puckered up and brought my lips close to the mirror, trying to see how I would look to any potential kissee. But I never tried it with a girl.

On the first day of camp, the guys from my cabin gathered on the lawn and began making informal bets with each other about who would be able to kiss which girl. I listened raptly to all predictions. I was full of questions like, how do you know she'll let you kiss her? And, must you wait until it's dark or can you kiss in the daylight? I didn't ask any of the questions because I didn't want to look like the only one there with no kissing experience.

Fortunately, there was another kid, Jamie, who wasn't afraid to ask. He got right to the heart of things and asked important stuff like, "Should I lick my lips first, so they're moist?" and "Where do I put my hands?" I hung on the answers to Jamie's questions.

It was unanimously agreed that we would be The Kissing Cabin. We made a solemn pact. Each of us would attempt to kiss a girl at least once a day, each and every day of camp. It didn't have to be a different girl every day, but we did have to try for a kiss. We figured it out mathematically. There were nine of us in the cabin and camp lasted seven days. If each of us fulfilled the pact, that would be sixty-three kisses. Everyone except Jamie and me seemed confident that they could manage more than one kiss per day, especially toward the end of the week. The possibilities were staggering. We upped the goal from sixty-three to one-hundred.

For the rest of the week, I was obsessed with trying to kiss a girl. First I had to talk to one. I hung around the snack shop, but the girls came in groups and I was too intimidated to talk to them collectively. Then I tried strolling along the lake shore. My plan was to say "hi" to any girl who was also strolling. I only met one. I said, "Hi." She said, "Hi." I didn't know what else to say. I *wanted* to say, "Do you mind if I kiss you?", but I didn't have the nerve. So I kept walking and so did she and that was the end of that.

At the end of the first day, we gathered to begin the official score keeping. Three of the nine guys had already managed a kiss. One of them had five kisses to his credit. Five! It was clear that I would need to do more than stroll along the lake shore and mumble, "Hi."

By the end of the third day, Jamie and I were the only ones who had nothing to report. Even without us, the score was an impressive thirty-six.

My opportunity finally came on day five, when I had nearly given up hope. Ironically, it happened in religion class. I arrived late and the only empty chair was in the back row. I tiptoed in, sat down, and smiled at the girl beside me. She smiled back.

Inspired by such encouragement, I opened my notebook and began writing. I asked her name. She wrote, "Jean." I wrote, "Pretty name. Pretty girl." She smiled again. We scribbled notes all through class and then when I handed her the pencil, our hands touched and neither of us pulled away.

My heart started to pound. I wasn't even thinking about the

guys in the Kissing Cabin or about our goal for the week. All I was thinking about was how Jean's hair curled around her shoulders and how soft her hand felt against mine.

Religion class always ended with a prayer. That day, when the prayer began, I realized that all the leaders had their eyes closed. Jean and I were in the back row, where none of the other campers could see us.

Cautiously, I opened one eye and peeked at Jean. She was watching me. My fingers squeezed hers and then I leaned toward her. Our lips met seconds before the "Amen."

By the close of camp, the Kissing Cabin had surpassed its goal. Final count was one-hundred fourteen, but that didn't include any goodby kisses that were collected as we waited in line to board the buses. My personal contribution to the total was twelve kisses, all of them with Jean.

My parents were waiting at the bus depot to pick me up.

"Did you have fun?" my mother asked anxiously. I assured her that I had enjoyed myself.

"Did you learn anything?" my dad asked.

"More than I expected," I said. "Especially about the beauty of nature."

#28

Locker Room Lessons

There's a community swimming pool in our town and every summer my friends and I swim there. My parents encourage me to go because they want me to learn how to swim. I *have* learned a lot at the pool, but most of what I've learned doesn't have anything to do with swimming.

For example, the locker room of the pool is where I first learned that adults have pubic hair. I tried not to stare at people when they were dressing, but it was impossible not to notice something so obvious.

I also learned at the pool that not everyone is as honest as they should be. My parents always give me a dollar to go swimming — seventy-five cents admission and twenty-five cents to rent a locker to put my things in while I am in the water. It didn't take me long to figure out that if I didn't rent a locker, I had twenty-five cents to spend on candy on the way home. You can't buy much for a quarter, but twenty-five cents worth of gummie bears is better than no gummie bears at all. So I always left my clothes and my towel in a pile on a bench in the locker room.

One day, when I dripped into the locker room, ready to get dressed, buy my gummie bears, and head for home, my towel was gone. So were my shoes! And so was the twenty-five cents which had been in the pocket of my jeans.

I was outraged. The twenty-five cents was bad enough, but who would take my shoes? I knew my parents wouldn't be pleased that the towel was missing either. The worst part was admitting that I had spent the money on candy all along, rather than renting a locker.

One summer, my friend Billy, learned to dive. Billy took swimming lessons when he visited his grandparents for a month, and when he returned he knew how to dive. He taught me how and we took turns diving off the low board.

One day Billy announced that he was going to dive off the high board. I watched as he cimbed up the ladder. He walked to the end of the board, jumped up and down a couple of times, and flew off, with his arms aimed toward the water and his toes pointed to the sky. It looked easy. Billy surfaced, swam to the side, and went right back up the ladder to do it again.

He urged me to dive off the high board too. I hesitated. The truth is, I can't even look down when I'm driving across a bridge in a car. And stairways where I can see between the stairs always make my knees tremble. I wasn't so sure I wanted to climb that ladder.

But Billy kept saying there was nothing to it and I didn't want him to think I was chicken, so finally I agreed to give it a try. I started up the ladder. Part way up, I stopped and looked down. I would have backed up right then except there were two other kids climbing the ladder behind me and they said to hurry.

I swallowed hard, looked at the rung above me, and kept going. When I got to the top of the ladder, I stepped out onto the diving board. It was not a narrow diving board. There was plenty of room for me to walk, but I felt as if I were trying to balance on a tightrope.

I made it to the end of the board and gave a tentative bounce. As I did, I looked down at the water and began to sweat. My knees got shaky and my throat felt all tight, like it did when I had the mumps.

I couldn't do it. Not only was I incapable of diving head first off the high board, I was not capable of jumping off, either. I couldn't even turn around and walk away. I dropped to my knees and crawled back to the ladder.

The kid behind me had to step over me and two others had to back down the ladder to let me off.

I was humiliated, but I learned something from the ordeal. I learned I should trust my instincts and not make myself do something I didn't want to do, just because somebody else thought it was fun.

I staggered into the locker room, with my head down; Billy followed me. When someone asked what was wrong, Billy said I'd had a little too much sun. He never told anybody what had happened, which taught me something about friendship.

As I said, I've learned a lot of useful things at the pool. And most of them had nothing to do with swimming.

#29

I Bequeath to Eddie My Model Rockets

Last week my parents each made a will. For days they debated how to handle their property and personal belongings, in case they should die together. They discussed who would get their computer and who would get all Dad's darkroom equipment and who would get Mom's jewelry.

Since I'm an only child, they said I would inherit most of their estate, but there were a few other people whom they wanted to remember with personal belongings.

It made me nervous to hear them talk like that. I know that in the normal course of events, I will probably out-live my parents, but they were talking as if it could happen tomorrow. That's scary. Although it isn't likely to happen tomorrow, it *could*.

I haven't had much experience with death. My grandpa died when I was six, but he lived far away and I didn't see him often enough to feel close to him. The worst part about Grandpa's death was seeing my dad cry.

My cat died last year. I cried over him and I still miss him, but his death didn't change my life much. Losing my parents would make a change. A huge change.

While Mom and Dad talked about willing their possessions, I clowned around and acted greedy. I said I want the computer and the stereo and the VCR with the remote control. And the new car. I definitely want the new car.

Dad said if he willed all that to me, he'd be afraid of getting arsenic in his granola some morning because I wouldn't be able to wait.

Now the truth is, I'd love to have a car of my own. Any car. I'd love to have my own computer too, but I wouldn't want a computer or a car if the only way to get them was to lose my parents. Mom and Dad know that; that's why we could kid around about it.

I told them if they were going to make a list of who gets their personal possessions, I had better do the same, in case I came down with a terminal head cold, or got run over by a cement truck. That night I read them my will. They got all my bedroom furniture, which only seemed fair, since they paid for all of it. I willed my baseball card collection to my cousin, Jamie, and my new running shoes to my friend, Brendan. My model rockets go to Brendan's little brother, Eddie.

I had fun making my will. I knew how happy Jamie and Brendan and Eddie would be to get my things. Especially Eddie. Eddie has always wanted to shoot off one of my model rockets, but Brendan and I never let him do it.

I wondered if my friends would feel about my treasures the way I feel about Mom and Dad's possessions. Would Jamie rather have me in person, or inherit my baseball cards? Too bad I wouldn't be around to see their reactions.

I didn't tell anyone except Mom and Dad about my will. For one thing, I don't want to start any rumors that I am suicidal. For another, the items in my will probably won't last as long as I do. My running shoes will get old and scuffed and my model rockets may crash and break. I'll have to make a whole new will next year.

The baseball cards should increase in value, but I may change my mind about leaving them to Jamie. If my folks let me get a dog, like I hope they do, I may change my will and have all my possessions sold with the proceeds going to a trust fund to buy dog food.

Even though Mom and Dad and I intend to live for a long time, making the wills changed us. We're more patient with each other now and less critical. It used to bother me that Dad's hairstyle is hopelessly out of date, but now it doesn't matter. Mom's quit nagging me to eat more vegetables. Somehow, when we contemplated the possibility of losing each other, it made us value our time together more.

It also made me realize that possessions are only things and things are never as important as people. Tomorrow I'm going to let Eddie shoot off one of my model rockets. What the heck. I may as well have the fun of watching him.

#30

Delivering Pizza Is Never Dull

I thought delivering pizzas would be boring. I expected to drive around town, deliver the pizzas and collect the money. Not much to tell my friends about.

I started the job last night. As I drove to the first address on my list, I practiced what I was supposed to say when the person came to the door: "Tony's Pizza. Your hot pizza is here."

I found the house, carried the box of pizza to the door, and rang the bell.

A naked woman answered. I tried not to stare but it wasn't easy. I swallowed hard, handed her the box, and stammered, "Pony's Teatsa. Your hot skin . . . uh, your hot order is here."

The naked woman gave me a funny look. Then she said I should come in because she had to find her purse. I said I was supposed to wait outside. There's no way I was going in that house. When she returned with the money, she looked at me funny again and said the pizza was bigger than she expected and she'd be glad to share it if I wanted to help her eat it.

I finally caught on and realized she wanted to share more than the pizza. My palms started to sweat. A guy like me always dreams of how it would be to have women chase him, but I never expected it to happen. Certainly not when I was delivering a pepperoni pizza.

I told her I was sorry, but I had another pizza to deliver and I didn't want it to get cold. Then I beat it out of there.

At the next house, four guys were playing poker. Empty beer cans littered the floor and it was obvious by the way the men acted that two were winning and two were losing. The two losers snarled at me and glowered at their cards. One of the winners paid for the pizza and told me to keep the change.

I looked at the bill he gave me. It was a fifty. The pizza

came to $16.95. If he gave me a twenty, it would be a generous tip. I told him I thought he'd made a mistake.

"It's no mistake," he said. "I've got plenty more where that came from."

The two surly looking men glared at me and started muttering how it came from their pockets, so I shoved the fifty in my own pocket and left.

I got to the third address on my list, took a deep breath, and wondered what I'd find behind the door this time. A man peeked out and asked how much. I told him the cost of the pizza, he gave me the money, took the pizza, and quickly shut the door. I sighed with relief as I drove away. At last. A boring house.

Two blocks later, police cars converged on me. When I pulled over, four police officers ordered me to get out and put my hands on top of the truck. One of them held a gun on me while the others searched me.

My mind raced, trying to figure out what I had done. I knew I wasn't speeding and I didn't think I'd missed a stop sign. The only thing I could think of was the naked lady. Had she been so insulted by my refusal to join her that she made up some story about me and called the police?

"Did you stop me because of the naked woman?" I asked.

One of the officers said, "Naked women, too? This case may be bigger than we thought."

After they searched me, they searched my truck. I told them if they were looking for pizza they were too late because I'd made all my deliveries and was on my way back to the shop.

They let me go without explaining anything. This morning I learned they weren't looking for pizza. They were looking for drugs. The boring house was the site of a big drug bust late last night. It was already staked out when I arrived. The cops saw me go to the door, hand something inside, take money in return, and leave. I can't blame them for being suspicious.

There was a picture of the house in the morning paper. The narcotics squad found $80,000 worth of cocaine in the bedroom and a marijuana greenhouse in the basement.

My name wasn't in the paper this time, but it might be tomorrow. With an exciting job like mine, anything can happen.

#31

I Hate My Middle Name

The first time I heard my middle name, I hated it. Zippthorne. Zippthorne! Spelled with two P's. I don't know what my parents were thinking of when they hung that handle on me. They weren't thinking of my future happiness, that's for sure.

It wouldn't be so bad if Zippthorne was a cherished family name, something that went back several generations. If I had a kindly Grandma Zippthorne who read stories to me when I was little, and let me eat peanut butter cookies before dinner, I'd feel a nostalgic loyalty to the name.

It would be better yet if the Zippthornes were rich philanthropists, known and respected throughout the state. If Great-grandfather Zippthorne was a wealthy industrialist, and there was a huge Zippthorne office building downtown, and a Zippthorne Park, and maybe a Zippthorne Memorial Opera House, I would be proud of my middle name.

There is no such connection. On the night I was born, my parents ran out of gas on the way to the hospital. My dad started off on foot to get some gasoline, leaving my mother in the car. A young couple came along, stopped to see if Mom needed help, and drove her to the hospital. She said they joked and laughed all the way and helped her relax. When she asked their names, the young man said, "Zippthorne," and my mother decided she would name her baby after him.

I'm dead certain he just made that name up on the spur of the moment. He was clowning around and out popped, "Zippthorne." Mom admits that the young woman went into peals of laughter after the man gave his name.

Nonetheless, Mom was true to her word. When I was born an hour later, my middle name became Zippthorne. My mother never saw the couple again, and when she looked up Zippthorne in the telephone directory, there wasn't any listing.

I believe my middle name is the product of a young man's imagination, a foolish spontaneous answer that was intended as a joke. My mother staunchly insists that I'm named after a kind-hearted samaritan with a sense of humor.

Regardless of the man's sterling qualities, throughout my childhood I wished Mother had never met him. If other kids found out what the "Z" stood for, they'd hoot and holler. "Zippthorne?" they'd say. "You're kidding. C'mon, what's your real middle name?"

When I insisted that Zippthorne was really it, they couldn't wait to tell someone else. Like a funny joke, the news of an outrageous middle name travels swiftly on the school yard grapevine.

And then someone invariably called me Zippy. I can't think of a worse nickname than Zippy. It sounds like a device used to close a pair of trousers.

I'm not the only person with this problem. Lots of people hate their middle names. Some hate their middle names so much that they refuse ever to use them, going only by the initial.

I think parents have entirely too much say in the naming of children, and I've developed a plan which would eliminate a lot of unhappiness about names. With my plan, the names which parents choose for their infants would be Ten Year Names. It would be understood by everyone that at the age of ten, each person gets to select a new name. This, too, would be a Ten Year Name, because some kids of ten wouldn't be any better at selecting a decent name than their parents were. The final, permanent name would be chosen at age twenty, when each person can either keep the same name he chose at age ten, or make one more change.

My plan would prevent ridicule of kids by other kids, and would eliminate feelings of resentment toward parents.

After I told my parents about my plan, they said if I'm truly unhappy with Zippthorne, I can pick out a new middle name and use it. They said for my birthday they will pay the fees to make the change legal.

I spent weeks writing lists of names. First I chose Brad. Short and simple. I'd never have to spell my middle name again. But then I met someone named Brad that I didn't like, so I changed my mind and chose Paul. The first time I told someone my middle name was Paul, he said that was his middle name, too. I started realizing how many Pauls there are. It's a nice, solid name, but it isn't at all unusual.

Despite its drawbacks, I enjoy having a middle name that nobody else has. I began asking everyone I knew what their middle name was. Soon I had a lengthy list, with everything from Aaron to Zachary. But there was no Zippthorne. Not a single one. So I decided to keep the middle name I've always had. Zippthorne. Spelled with two P's.

#32

The Wishbone

Most of the time I like my brother. Twice a year, on Thanksgiving and New Year's Day, I don't like him. Those are the days when my mother cooks a turkey dinner, and Robbie and I get to wish on the wishbone.

Robbie always wins. He's three years older than I, and stronger, and when we each grasp one side of the wishbone and pull, my side always breaks. Always.

I've tried not pulling. I've tried pulling with all my strength. I've tried a sudden, intense jerk, and I've tried a slow, steady drag. No matter what strategy I use, Robbie ends up with the big part of the wishbone and I end up with a small, splintered end.

The problem isn't the wishbone itself; it's the magic. A wish made on a wishbone will come true. That is, it will come true for the person who wins the wishbone tug.

My wish is always the same: to make the honor roll. I'm an average student. I never flunk anything, but I don't get A's either. I get mostly C's, with a B in physical education. To be on the honor roll, it's necessary to have a B average. Every time I hold my half of the wishbone, I wish that my grades would be good enough, just once, to put me on the honor roll.

Robbie will never tell me what he wished for. He says if you tell your wish, it won't come true. He claims that every Thanksgiving and every New Year's Day, the wish that he made on the wishbone has really happened. He swears it!

Once I asked him to prove it. He made a list, going back four years, of things he wished for. All of them came true. According to Robbie's list, he wished for cowboy boots one Thanksgiving and two weeks later, for his birthday, he got them. Another time he wished to get a part-time job and within a month he was hired to work Saturdays at Taco Time.

When I told my friend, Arnold, about the list, he pointed out that Robbie might have made up the list, using things that had actually happened. He said there was no way to prove that Robbie really wished for cowboy boots and a job.

I knew Arnold was right, but deep down I still believed that if only I could win the wishbone war, just once, I'd bring home an honor roll report card.

Last fall a new girl came to my school. Margie is the prettiest girl I ever met and the nicest. And the smartest. Margie's a real brain, and I knew she'd never notice me unless my grades improved drastically.

I started studying for an extra hour every night. I brought home my math assignments, even if I finished them in class. I went over them again at home to be sure I caught any mistakes. When my English teacher offered extra credit for book reports, I read three books and wrote reports on them.

I asked Arnold to quiz me before we had a history test. We made up cue cards and used them together and we were the only two in the class who got one hundred percent. After class, Margie smiled at me and said, "Congratulations." It was the first time she ever spoke to me. From then on, Arnold and I made cue cards and practiced for every history test. We didn't always get one hundred, but we never got below ninety, which is a whole lot better than I ever did in history before.

I worked on my science project every weekend, instead of waiting until the day before it was due, and then trying to throw a project together.

Something amazing happened on Thanksgiving. After we ate our turkey dinner, Robbie and I grabbed the wishbone, and for the first time ever, his side snapped. I won!

I stared at the winning portion of the wishbone in disbelief. I'd lost so many times, I had given up hope of ever winning.

Robbie asked me what my wish was, but I refused to tell. Naturally, I wished the same thing I'd wished all those other times — to make the honor roll.

When report cards came out the middle of December, I was almost afraid to look. What if the magic hadn't worked? I didn't need to worry. I not only made the honor roll; I made the Dean's List. Two B's and three A's.

Those wishbones are even more powerful than I realized.

#33

The House I Used to Live In

For the first ten years of my life, I lived in a big brown shingle house. It had a huge front yard. We used to play baseball in that front yard. My friends, Brian and Kelly, who lived in the same block, came over every day and we used a big red plastic baseball bat and a plastic baseball.

The batter's box was right between two rose bushes, next to the sidewalk. First base was under the living room window. Second base was at Mrs. O'Neill's driveway, which was the property line. Third base was under the elm tree.

I can remember whacking that baseball clear into Mrs. O'Neill's yard and racing from the window to the driveway to the elm tree and back to the rose bushes. A homerun! My heart pounded with the joy of it. I knew that any kid who could hit homeruns like that was headed for a career in the major leagues. Today, a brown shingle house; tomorrow, Candlestick Park.

Brian and Kelly both lived on the other side of the street. You had to climb steps to get to their houses, and the yards weren't big enough to play baseball in. I always felt lucky that I had such a big front yard — as big as a baseball field.

We moved to a different town when I was ten, but I never forgot the brown shingle house. It was the house where I learned to ride a bike and where I started school and where the Cub Scouts came every Wednesday afternoon to work on crafts and learn songs and eat cookies.

That's where we lived when I stopped being an only child and became an older brother. It's the house where we put on plays in the basement and ran through the sprinkler in our bathing suits. It's where we roasted hot dogs in the fireplace in January and sat on a blanket on the floor to eat them, and called it a winter picnic.

After we moved, I wrote to Brian and Kelly once, but they never answered. I made new friends. Letter writing was never high on my list of Things I Like To Do.

I liked our next house a lot. It was newer and had a sliding glass door that opened onto a patio. In that house, I learned to play the trumpet and made the school basketball team and grew four inches in one year. I learned to use a computer and speak French. I discovered that I was good at algebra.

Last year we took a vacation and went back to the town where I was born. I wanted to go back and look at our old house. As we turned on to the street, I kept expecting to see Brian and Kelly, both still ten years old, waving to me from their yards.

When we stopped in front of our old house, I was stunned. The brown shingles were still brown, the rose bushes were still blooming next to the sidewalk, and Mrs. O'Neill's driveway was exactly where it always was. But the space within those landmarks had shrunk. The front yard was small! It wasn't even an average-sized city lot; it was tiny!

In my mind, I could see home plate, and the three bases, but in between them, there was hardly any room to run. Twelve feet, at the most. How could I have thought, for all those years, that I had a huge front yard?

Now I wish I hadn't gone back to see the old house. I liked it better when it had a front yard the size of a baseball diamond, where a small boy could hit a homerun with a red plastic bat and believe he was only a step away from a major league career.

#34

Tale of a Lost Dog

Because of my sister's allergies, my family has no pets. Therefore, I was surprised to find muddy paw prints on the kitchen floor one morning. They led from the back door, through the kitchen, down the hallway, and into my bedroom closet.

When I opened the closet door, I found Sissy crouched on the floor, clutching a muddy yellow dog. The dog's tail waved back and forth across my clean clothes.

"What are you doing?" I demanded.

"Shhh!" she said and motioned for me to join them in the closet.

"You're going to have an asthma attack," I said, as I squeezed in beside her and shut the door. "You know you can't touch dog fur."

"I'm saving his life," she hissed. "The dog catcher's truck is on our street and nobody knows where this dog belongs."

Shllurp. A wet tongue caressed my cheek. It was impossible to be certain in the dark, but I assumed the tongue belonged to the dog and not my sister.

"He needs our help," Sissy declared. "Without us, he's a goner, for sure."

Shllurp. The other cheek got it.

I wiped my face on the back of my hand and tried to think. We couldn't keep the dog in my closet. We couldn't keep the dog anywhere, not with Sissy's allergies.

"I'll stay here with the dog," I said. "You go see if you can find where he belongs."

A low whimpering began. It was not the dog. "I can't leave him," Sissy blubbered. "He needs me."

I eased back out of the closet and set off. No one in the neighborhood was missing a dog. No one knew any medium-sized yellow dog, missing or not.

I saw Frankie Hatchem in front of the drug store. Frankie had a remote control model airplane that I had coveted for weeks. I'd tried several times to trade something for it, but the only thing I had that Frankie wanted was my football which was autographed by seven members of the Denver Broncos. I would rather part with an arm than give up my football.

In a flash of inspiration, I said, "Hey, Frankie. Would you trade your model airplane for a dog?"

Frankie looked suspicious. "What kind of dog?" he asked. "Where's the dog? I don't see any dog."

"My sister has the dog," I told him, "but she can't keep it because she's allergic to dog fur." That was the truth. "It's a real loving dog," I added.

"Is it a boy or a girl?" Frankie asked.

"Boy," I said. I figured I had a fifty-fifty chance of being right.

"I'd have to ask my Ma," Frankie said.

I know Frankie's ma. She laughs a lot and doesn't get mad when Frankie and I make a mess. I figured she was a shoe-in for a homeless dog.

I was right. Within half an hour, Frankie was at my house with his model airplane. It was none too soon. I could hear Sissy sneezing in the closet. Fortunately, Mom wasn't home.

I opened the closet door and Muddy Yellow wagged his tail at Frankie. That's all it took. Frankie handed over the airplane, and took Muddy Yellow home with him.

The next day I took my new airplane to the park and flew it. I should have asked Frankie to go with me, to explain how everything worked. I figured out how to turn the controls to "on" and I got the plane in the air, but then I didn't know how to land it again. It went faster and faster, flying erratically up, down and sideways while I alternately pushed and pulled on the steering knob. The plane dove downward, dangerously close to a parked car. I panicked, hit the switch and the plane careened out of control and smashed into the parking lot.

I gathered up the parts, put them in my backpack and trudged home. When I got there, a furious Frankie was waiting on my front porch.

"That dog already had an owner," he said. "There was a 'LOST' ad in the newspaper last night and my parents made me call the number. The people came right over and got him." Frankie glared at me. "Our deal's off," he said. "I want my model airplane back."

When I opened the backpack and took out the pieces, Frankie started yelling at me, and the only way I could keep him from telling my parents about the dog was to give him the autographed football.

So Frankie got my football, Sissy got an asthma attack, and I got in trouble because Frankie's ma saw my mom at the grocery store and blabbed the whole story.

Later I found out that the dog's owner had offered a reward, but Frankie's ma wouldn't let him take it. It hardly seems fair. I deserved a reward, but all I got out of the deal was a broken model airplane.

#35

The Stupidest Thing I Ever Did

I have done many stupid things in my life, but the most stupid of all was something I did when I was nine. My brother was three years old that year and he nearly drove me crazy. Everything I did, Benny wanted to do, too. When my friends came over, Benny hung around and tried to play with us. It was embarrassing. Who wants to come over and play if a bratty three-year-old has to be included in everything?

The worst part of all was that when I did anything wrong, I always got in big trouble. But when Benny did anything wrong, Mom always made excuses.

For example, when I put the hole in my bedroom wall, I was grounded for a whole week. And the hole wasn't even my fault. I was practicing my batting stance and I put a weight on the baseball bat and then I swung the bat and the weight flew off and went right through the wall. It hardly seems fair to get grounded for something that was clearly an accident. Mom said I knew better than to practice batting indoors.

The very next day, Benny spilled a bottle of shampoo. Then he got the vacuum cleaner, turned it on and vacuumed up all the shampoo. It completely ruined the inside of the vacuum cleaner, but did he get punished? No way. All Mom said was, "He's only three; he didn't know any better."

And that's when I decided to get Benny in big trouble, which, as it turned out, was the most stupid decision of my life.

I thought and thought, trying to think what Benny could do that would make Mom absolutely furious. It had to be something so terrible that she would completely blow her stack.

The idea came to me in school the next day. I was sitting at my desk, tracing my finger along all the names that people had carved into the desk over the years when suddenly I knew what I would do.

As soon as I got home that day, I went to the kitchen and sneaked a small, sharp paring knife out of the drawer. I waited until Mom was talking on the telephone and then I went into the living room and looked around.

Our piano used to belong to my grandmother. It's made of rosewood, it's more than sixty years old, and it has been in our family since it was new. I sat on the piano bench and stared at the piano. It was beautiful wood, much nicer than my desk at school. Then I thought about all the times Benny had bothered me and my friends and how he never gets punished.

I used the tip of the knife and, on the front of the piano, right over the keys, I carved Benny's name. I made big letters, about three inches high. B-E-N-N-Y.

When I walked across the room and looked at the piano. Benny's name showed up clearly, from every angle.

I slipped the knife back into the drawer and waited for Mom to scream at Benny. But she didn't go into the living room and finally I couldn't stand to wait any longer. I went to Mom and asked her if she had seen what Benny did to the piano.

Mom took one look and blew her stack. I knew she'd get angry, but I didn't know she'd be completely out of control. I was grounded for a whole month, and half my allowance each week for an entire year went toward the cost of having the piano refinished.

When I said it wasn't fair to punish me for something Benny did, Mom pointed out that Benny was only three and did not yet know how to write his name. And that's when I knew I had done the most stupid thing of my entire life.

#36

The Day I Was a Hero

The day I was a hero began like any ordinary day. It was a Saturday and as soon as I finished cleaning my room, I got on my bike and started pedaling toward the hobby store. I'd saved my allowance for three weeks and finally had enough to buy the new car I wanted for my train set. It's a coal car, filled with little black lumps that look like real coal.

On my way to the hobby store, I crossed a railroad track. Since it was after ten and the daily train goes by at ten-thirty, I decided to wait for it. Maybe there would be a real coal car on it and I could see what it looked like up close.

I leaned my bike against a tree and sat down in the grass to wait for the train. No matter how many times I watched the train go by, it was always exciting. I could feel the ground shake and hear the shrill whistle blow, even before the engine came around the bend, into view.

While I waited, I felt in my pocket, to be sure my money was still there. It was. Fifteen dollars and thirty-one cents. As I counted it, I remembered seeing a penny once that was flattened out to twice its normal diameter. The man who showed it to me told me that it was run over by a train. I wondered if my penny would get big and flat like that, if the train ran over it. I decided to find out.

I placed my penny carefully on the rail. It was a new penny and the copper gleamed bright in the late morning sunshine. I hoped the engineer wouldn't see it and stop the train.

I wondered if it was illegal to put a penny on the railroad tracks. I didn't think it would hurt the train, but a penny is government property, and I didn't want to go to jail for destroying government property.

I decided it would be wise to stay out of sight until the train was past. I moved my bike, hiding it carefully in a clump of bushes. Then I climbed the maple tree, which gave me a good vantage point. I could see my penny and the oncoming train, but I was out of sight.

I had been in the tree for only a few minutes when I heard a noise. Looking down through the branches, I recognized Danny Thorgelson. He was walking along, throwing rocks at the railroad ties. Danny Thorgelson is a real creep and I was glad I was hidden in the tree where he couldn't see me.

He bent down, scooped up more rocks and flung them, one at a time, at the rails. One of them landed beside my penny. Danny stopped and looked and I knew he'd seen my penny.

Just then, the trian whistle blew and the ground started to shake. I saw Danny hesitate. I knew he wanted the penny, but he couldn't tell how close the train was.

I yelled down out of the tree. "That's my penny, Creep, so stay away from it."

Danny jumped and looked up. When he saw it was me in the tree, he said, "Finders, keepers." Then he threw a rock into the branches. Fortunately, it missed me.

I glared down at him. The whistle shrieked again and the engine chugged around the bend. I crouched on my tree limb, ready to spring. I figured Danny would wait until the train passed and then try to grab my flattened penny and run. I planned to jump him as soon as the train was by us, before he could get to the penny.

Danny didn't wait. When the train was less than a block away, he lunged forward toward the penny. The train loomed closer. The engineer must have seen Danny because the whistle started going off like crazy.

I jumped off the branch. The idea of creepy Danny Thorgelson getting away with my penny made me so angry that I didn't stop to think. I leaped out of that tree and landed on Danny's back just before his hand reached the penny.

I hit him with such force that it knocked him across the

tracks and into the gravel on the other side. I came down on top of him, and lay there, my heart pounding, as the train rumbled past with its brakes squealing.

When it stopped, people climbed out to see if we were all right. The police arrived. So did an ambulance and a reporter from the local newspaper. Danny was knocked unconscious and had to go to the hospital.

I wasn't hurt. Danny cushioned my fall.

The newspaper reporter talked to the engineer and other men on the train. They agreed they were going to hit Danny and then, at the last second, I knocked him out of the way. They said I saved Danny's life.

The reporter only asked me one question; he wanted to know if I stopped to think, before I jumped, that I might get killed. I said, "No."

I got my picture in the paper and there was a big story with the headline: YOUNG HERO SAVES CLASSMATE FROM CERTAIN DEATH. The story told how I jumped from the tree in a selfless attempt to save another person's life. It also said the police found a flattened penny on the track after the train moved and they speculated that Danny was putting it there when I saved him.

It turned out that Danny only had a mild concussion. He was released from the hospital the next day. When he saw the newspaper story, he was furious.

I got a certificate from the railroad company, honoring me for my heroic act. I didn't get my penny back, though. Somehow, I thought it was best not to ask for it.

Part Three:

MONOLOGS
FOR
BOYS OR GIRLS

#37

Never Kiss a Shedding Cat

Medical research shows that people who own pets have fewer medical problems. It is relaxing to own a pet; stroking their fur lowers your blood pressure. Because pet owners feel needed, they are less prone to depression.

I don't like to argue with qualified researchers, but the truth is, I personally would be healthier if I didn't have a pet. I know for certain that I'd get more sleep.

I own a cat. Or, rather, my cat owns me. There's not much doubt about which of us runs the show.

Her name is Dolly and she's a fine, portly pussy. She did not develop her stout figure on a starvation diet. When Dolly is hungry, she lets me know and I feed her. The time of day — or night — is immaterial.

Dolly knows several ways to let me know when she is hungry. If it's daylight time, she simply comes up to me and yowls. Straightforward and effective.

If it's three a.m., and I am sound asleep, she has different strategies. The first is to lie on my bedroom floor, put one paw under the closet door, and pull just enough to make the door rattle. This can be repeated several times, alternating paws, if necessary. The only sure way to make her stop is to throw my pillow at her — but then I'm left without a pillow and can't get back to sleep. Usually, I try to ignore the rattling door — hoping she'll tire of it and go away.

It is useless to try to solve the problem by shutting Dolly out of the bedroom. She will only lie on the floor in the hall, put her paws under the *bedroom* door and rattle it.

If the rattling closet door fails to rouse me, the next step is to stand on her hind legs and scratch on the side of my mattress with her front claws. This tactic is somewhat risky because I can swat at her with my pillow without letting go of the pillow. She scampers away and I go back to sleep.

But not for long. When rattling the door and scratching the mattress fail to achieve results, Dolly proceeds to Plan Three: jump up on the dresser and knock things off. Coins work well. They are easily moved with one paw and they make a satisfying "clink" as they land on the floor and roll away. If the coins don't do the trick, she will push off a pencil, belt buckle or wallet.

It is impossible to sleep when my worldly possessions are dropping, one by one, off the top of the dresser. I get up and feed the cat.

I have tried putting cat food out before I go to bed. This only postpones the agony. If the food is there at bedtime, Dolly does not save it for three a.m. She eats it at bedtime. This does keep her from getting hungry and awakening me at three. Instead, she gets hungry and awakens me at five, which is even worse. If I have to get up at three a.m., I can usually go right back to sleep. When I have to get up at five a.m., I go back to bed and stare at the ceiling because I know my alarm is going to ring in only one hour.

Besides the sleep deprivation, owning a cat is hazardous to my health in other ways. There is the mental strain and stress that comes from worrying how I am going to pay the veterinarian after Dolly has a fight with the neighbor cat, and develops an abscess on her ear. There is also the stress of having to apologize to the neighbors because Dolly started the fight on *their* property.

There are compensations, of course. Dolly has a fine, loud purr which is instantly activated whenever she is petted. She is an excellent mouser, though I wish she didn't feel compelled to bring her trophies home and consume them on the front steps. She is soft and cuddly and likes to be a lap cat. I have to use caution, though. Because she is so soft, it's tempting to bury my face in her fur and nuzzle her. I have learned not to inhale at such times. Cat fur tickles the inside of my nose and is difficult to remove from my lips.

Once I gave Dolly a friendly nuzzle and nearly choked to death before I could get the excess fur out of my mouth.

I wonder if anyone has ever died from kissing a shedding cat. The researchers probably didn't think of that.

#38

I Caught Beethoven's Cold

Last week I had a terrible cold. My nose was stuffed up, my head ached, and I sounded like there was sandpaper between my tonsils. I spent two days lying around the house — drinking orange juice, taking aspirin, and feeling sorry for myself.

Now I feel fine. My head is clear, I no longer have a box of tissues under my arm, and my voice is back to normal. The cold is completely gone.

The question is: where did it go? A cold does not disappear like steam into the atmosphere. Nor does it put on a hat and exit, shutting the door behind it. No, colds sneak insidiously from one unsuspecting body to the next.

Sometimes I know where my colds come from. Over the years, I have caught my brother's cold, my uncle's cold, and the colds of various kids in my class. Once I caught the cold which belonged to the person standing behind me in line at the movie theatre. He sneezed six times before we got to the ticket window and the next day, my eyes started to water and my throat was scratchy.

The people who give me their colds don't mean to make me ill. It isn't really their fault, just as it isn't my fault that, no matter how careful I am to cover my mouth when I cough, I will pass my cold on to someone else.

I have given colds to my brother, my mother, my nursery school teacher, and several of my friends. Those are just the ones I know about for sure. There are probably dozens — maybe even hundreds — of other people who have caught cold from me without my knowing it. Once my brother and I passed a cold back and forth for six months, like a ping-pong game.

Even though I knew it wasn't transmitted on purpose, I used to get angry when I caught someone else's cold. I would wake up in the morning with a runny nose and I'd glare accusingly at my brother and say, "I caught your stupid cold." He, of course, would feel better by then which was proof that the cold had somehow left his body and entered mine.

Last week I decided to try to trace the origin of the cold I had. I thought it would be interesting to map its geneology and see how far back I could go. I would make a Sniffles and Sore Throat Family Tree.

I caught the cold from Eddie Klempton. Eddie sits next to me in history class, and he had the cold for several days before I came down with it. I asked Eddie if he knew where he caught it, and he said, sure, he caught it from his sister and his sister caught it from her boyfriend. He started to tell me, in vivid detail, exactly how his sister caught the cold from her boyfriend, but just as he got to the good part, our history teacher said if we didn't stop whispering and snickering, Eddie and I would both get an F for the week.

Eddie's sister's boyfriend hangs around with my brother, so I asked him where he had caught his cold. He thought he got it from a guy that his mother hired to paint their house. He couldn't remember the guy's name, so that was the end of this particular geneology.

The more I think about it, though, the more interesting it is to speculate on all the people through history who might have had the very same cold that I had last week.

It stands to reason that if a cold can go from person to person, time after time, then it can also go from generation to generation. People grow old and die, but colds just jump to a new body and keep on thriving.

My cold might very well have begun in another century. Maybe Abraham Lincoln had my cold. Maybe George Washington had my cold, and he gave it to Martha, and she gave it to Betsy Ross, and she gave it to a revolutionary soldier, and he gave it to the drummer boy.

Maybe Clark Gable had my cold.

The next time I catch cold, I'm not going to be angry at the person who had it just before I got it. Instead, I'll feel proud to be part of such a long and noble heritage. As I honk into my handkerchief, I'll reflect on all the famous people who might have passed that very cold on to me. Why, for all I know, I'm entrusted with Beethoven's germs.

#39

The Day I Switched
the Easter Eggs

Every year, my family colors Easter eggs. We hard-boil a couple of dozen eggs and we use little wire dippers to lower the eggs into cups filled with colored dye. On Easter morning, we put one egg by each person's plate and we eat the eggs for breakfast.

One Easter morning, many years back, my dad picked up his colored egg, leaned over to my mom, and cracked the egg on her head. He didn't hit her hard or anything — just enough to crack the hard-boiled egg. We kids thought it was the funniest thing we'd ever seen and the next year, on Easter morning, we begged him to do it again. Every year after that, Dad cracked his egg on Mom's head while she pretended to try to get away. Everyone always laughed, even Mom.

Then one year I switched the eggs. While we were coloring the hard-boiled eggs, I colored one that wasn't cooked. On Easter morning, I put my colored raw egg at Dad's place.

Naturally, everyone urged him to crack his egg on Mom's head, as usual, and she pretended she didn't want him to. Dad picked up the raw egg, reached over, and tapped the egg on top of Mom's head. The egg shell cracked open, spilling its contents into her hair.

Everyone sat in stunned silence, watching the raw egg slither down the side of Mom's head and plop onto her shoulder. Mom put her hand on her head and the smile disappeared from her face. As she blinked back tears, I remembered that she'd had her hair cut the day before — and paid extra for a shampoo and blow dry because she wanted to look her best for Easter.

Dad apologized like crazy and tried to wipe up the egg with his napkin. Then he glared at the rest of us. "If this is someone's idea of a joke," he said, "it isn't funny."

My sister said, "I didn't do it!"

"Neither did I!" said my brother.

All eyes turned toward me. "Maybe it was a mistake," I said. "Maybe one egg accidentally didn't get cooked."

Mom left the table and pretty soon I heard the shower turn on. The egg washed out OK, but by the time she dried her hair and got dressed again, it was too late to go to church. Breakfast wasn't much fun, either. The special Easter bread that Mom always bakes didn't taste as good as usual, and none of us even bothered to ask if we could eat our chocolate bunnies instead of drinking our orange juice.

After breakfast, Dad sent the other kids out of the kitchen. He turned to me and said, "That was a rotten thing to do to your mother."

I didn't say anything. I didn't want to admit my guilt, but I couldn't lie, either. I stared at the floor.

Dad said, "Every year, for at least ten years, we have laughed about cracking the Easter egg on Mom's head. She's always a good sport about it, and what started as a silly joke, became a family tradition. All of us looked forward to it every year, and now you've ruined it."

"It won't ever happen again," I said.

Dad said he was sure it wouldn't. But he also said he won't ever be able to crack an Easter egg on Mom's head again because from now on, instead of bringing back happy memories of silly times, it would bring back a sad memory of the morning when someone was unkind and spoiled everyone's fun.

I bit my lip. I didn't know what to say.

"Before you play another trick on someone," Dad said, "think of the consequences. Jokes are fun if they make everyone laugh. When they make people sad, they aren't jokes anymore."

I didn't get punished for what I did. But I'll never forget it. And I'll never play a trick on anyone without thinking about how *they* will feel.

What Dad said is true. Jokes are only fun if they make everyone laugh.

#40

In My Next Life I Hope
I'm a Hot Fudge Sundae

There's been a lot of talk lately about reincarnation. Some people pay for what they call, "past life regressions." They hope to find out who they were before they became who they are now.

The man who fixed our bathroom sink told us that he lived in Egypt more than two thousand years ago, and helped build one of the pyramids. I asked him what he did in the time between building the pyramids and becoming a plumber, but he didn't know.

While it would be interesting to know who I was in past lives, I'm more curious about who I might be in the future. If I am destined to be a rich, powerful person — the Queen *(King)* of England, for example, or the owner of Microsoft — I'd like to know it now so I can look forward to it. Maybe I could even arrange for a loan from a bank, to be paid off by the future me.

On the other hand, if I am scheduled to be an aphid or a cutworm the next time around, forever at the mercy of a dedicated gardener armed with pesticides, I would rather not know.

If I could be anything at all, I would want to be a hot fudge sundae. Hot fudge sundaes don't last too long, but while they are here, they bring pure pleasure. Everyone loves hot fudge sundaes. And I would be the elite of all hot fudge sundaes: large, cold scoops of rich vanilla ice cream — the expensive kind, made with eggs and a high percentage of butterfat.

My hot fudge sauce would be thick and creamy and there would be more than enough, so that whoever ate the sundae wouldn't run out of sauce before he ran out of ice cream.

There would be whipped cream on top — *real* whipped cream, not the kind that gets squirted out of a can. It would be whipped stiff and there would be a thick white glob of it.

Nuts are imperative, of course, but not the tiny pieces of chopped peanuts or walnuts that are so often sprinkled on a sundae. I will have whole cashews and pecans, lightly salted, and resting in the whipped cream. A bright red marachino cherry, with the stem still on, will be my crown.

Think what pleasure such a sundae would give to the person who was lucky enough to eat it. My mouth waters at the thought.

My sister says I can't do it. She says if I'm reincarnated, I have to come back as a person, not as a thing. She says I can't be a cutworm, either, because once I've reached a certain level of life I can't go back to a lower level. If she's right, I can quit worrying about the pesticide problem.

I'm not sure whether to believe her or not. I suspect in *her* past life, my sister was a slave trader or one of the ruthless rulers who dominated the peasants. Sis isn't known for her compassion, nor for her open mind.

Of course, there is no way to prove if she's right or wrong. There's no way to prove anything about reincarnation except maybe to die and I'm not in that much of a hurry to know the future. There are too many things I want to do in *this* life.

Like fix myself a genuine hot fudge sundae, with real whipped cream and whole cashews. Why stand here talking about my future lives when I could be making that sundae right now?

#41

Where's Sarah?

I was four years old when my sister, Sarah, was born. I was five when she died.

The months in between were happy months. Sarah and I shared a bedroom and I liked waking up and looking over at Sarah in her crib. If she was awake, we played peek-a-boo. I'd put my pillow in front of my face and say, "Where's Sarah?" Sarah would gurgle at me and I'd throw the pillow down and shout, "Peek-a-boo!" Then we'd giggle and do it again.

If she wasn't awake, I would climb out of my bed and go to her and put my hand through the slats of her crib.

"Hi, Sarah," I'd whisper. "Wake up and play with me." I would take her hand in mine and shake it, the way my papa shakes hands with his friends. Sarah always woke up when I did that, and then we'd play peek-a-boo until Mama came in.

One morning, when I shook Sarah's hand, she didn't wake up. Her hand felt cold, so I pulled her yellow blanket up around her shoulders. I crawled back into my own bed and waited. Every few minutes I called, "Where's Sarah?", but she just kept on sleeping.

After awhile, Mama came in. She smiled at me and said, "Good morning," before she bent over Sarah's crib.

Then Mama screamed. She screamed and screamed and I remember thinking that she shouldn't scream like that. She always told me to be quiet when Sarah was sleeping. She was going to wake the baby up herself with all that yelling.

Mama grabbed Sarah in her arms and ran out of the room. The look on her face scared me. I pulled the covers up over my head and tried not to listen.

A long time later, Papa came into my room and sat on the side of my bed. He told me he had some sad news for me. He pulled the covers down so he could see my face, and then he told me that Sarah had died and gone to heaven. Tears rolled down his cheeks and I stared at them. I had never seen Papa cry before.

I didn't know what "died" meant. I didn't know where heaven was. It amazed me that Mama and Papa would let Sarah go anywhere by herself. I wasn't even allowed to cross the street and I was much bigger than Sarah. I decided that when Sarah came back, I'd ask if I could go to heaven with her next time.

Only Sarah didn't come back. I waited and watched, but she never returned. Grandma and Grandpa came to visit. They hugged me and said how lucky they were to still have me. They cried when they said it and Mama cried, too.

The next morning when I woke up, Sarah's crib was still empty. I put on my wooly blue bathrobe and my bunny slippers, and I tiptoed downstairs and out the back door. I walked all around the yard, calling, "Sarah! Sarah?" I wondered why no one else was looking for her.

I didn't see how she could have gone very far. She didn't know how to walk yet. I thought she must be hiding somewhere. I worried that she would be hungry.

When Mama heard me calling for Sarah, she made me go inside. She explained that Sarah was dead. She told me Sarah would not come back. Not ever.

I listened to Mama's explanation. I didn't cry or argue or ask questions. I listened. But I didn't believe her.

Sarah not come back? It was unthinkable! She had to come back. Where else would she go?

The next week, Papa took Sarah's crib away and Mama packed all of Sarah's clothes in boxes. I wondered where Sarah would sleep and what she would wear when she came home.

As I grew older, I thought of Sarah less often. Months went by when I didn't think of her at all.

Eventually, of course, I understood what death meant. I accepted the fact that my sister would not return.

And yet, even now, so many years later, when I first wake

up in the morning, I sometimes look across the room, and in that hazy fog between sleep and awareness, I blink my eyes groggily and expect to see a baby in a crib, waiting to play peek-a-boo.

#42

My Favorite Food

I'm supposed to write a detailed description of my favorite food. It's an assignment for my English class.

My problem is that I can't decide which food is my favorite. First I thought I'd write about pizza. Deep dish pizza, with a thick, chewy crust. I always order a ground beef filling in a rich tomato sauce. I like extra cheese, too — mozzarella and Parmesan, and maybe a few chopped onions on top.

On the other hand, if I write about deep dish pizza, I won't be able to write about root beer floats. On a hot summer day, I'd choose a root bear float over deep dish pizza every time, especially if the root beer float is made properly. There is a trick to making *real* root beer floats. Many people don't know that. They think all you do is put some ice cream in a glass and pour root beer over the top. Not so.

First you put a tablespoon of ice cream — vanilla, of course — into the glass and add an inch of root beer. Mix this together thoroughly, so the ice cream is thoroughly blended. Then add two full scoops of ice cream and pour more root beer over the top. You'll need a straw, and a spoon with a long handle, and some extra root beer for refills.

When the temperature is over eighty degrees, nothing tastes better than a properly made root beer float.

But what about winter time? Even a perfect root beer float isn't appealing when there's snow on the ground. That's the time for homemade cinnamon rolls. My favorites are made with part white flour and part whole wheat flour so they have a wheat flavor and a kind of solid texture. They should be thick and high with generous amounts of melted butter, cinnamon and sugar between the layers — and a drizzle of white frosting on top. Served with a cold glass of milk, a warm homemade cinnamon roll is a feast fit for royalty.

There's only one trouble with writing about homemade cinnamon rolls. If I do that, I won't be able to write about caramel apples. There are few sensations in the world more pleasant than biting through a thick layer of chewy caramel, into a crisp, juicy apple. Once, when I was craving a caramel apple and didn't have one, I bought a bag of caramel candies and tried alternating bites of apple and candy. It wasn't the same. In order for it to taste exactly right, it is necessary to get both the caramel and the apple in the same bite. And the apple needs to be on a stick. Caramel apples are the perfect fall treat, but perhaps I shouldn't limit myself to a seasonal food. My assignment is to write about my favorite food and that should be something I eat all year long.

Blueberry pancakes. That's what I'll do. I'll write about blueberry pancakes. I can tell how we mix up the batter and stir in the plump, dark blueberries. You can tell when the griddle is hot enough by shaking a few drops of water on it. If the water dances around in little balls, the griddle is ready to fry the pancakes.

I drop blobs of batter and make animal shapes out of them. I have rabbit pancakes and cat pancakes. I make dog pancakes and elephant pancakes. My Dad always tries to cheat by saying he's going to make baseball pancakes, but I tell him that's too easy.

As the pancakes cook, little bubbles appear around the edges; juice oozes out of the blueberries and turns the batter purple. When the pancakes are flipped, they're golden brown on top with big blue dots where the berries are.

I stack them up on my plate, four high, and put butter in between them so it will melt. I like maple syrup on top, but blueberry syrup is good too. I think I could eat blueberry pancakes every single morning of my life and never get tired of them.

Still, I hesitate to call blueberry pancakes my favorite food. Maybe a favorite food should be something I get only on special occasions, something I look forward to, like the four-layer chocolate cake that my grandma always makes for my birthday. Or our homemade ice cream on the Fourth of July each year . . . or heart-shaped cookies for Valentine's Day or . . . excuse me. I think I'll write my report later. Right now, I need to get something to eat.

#43

When Some Day Comes

When some day comes, things will sure be different. My dad's going to clean out the garage some day, and my mom's going to actually make all those recipes that she keeps clipping out of magazines. One whole drawer in our kitchen is filled with recipes that she's going to try, "some day".

As for me, some day I'm going to quit eating junk food. It'll be "bye-bye Twinkies™; hello brussels sprouts." No more trading my carrot sticks for Ding-Dongs during lunch period. No more potato chips and cokes after school. I'll be bursting with vitamins.

When some day comes, all the roads in our town will be repaired. We'll be able to drive from our house to any place else without bouncing in potholes, or detouring, or waiting for construction equipment. Big signs that say, "Caution: Flag Man Ahead" will be things of the past. They may even become collectibles and sell for high prices in antique shops.

Some day my brothers will quit fighting and be civil to each other. At least, my mother says they will. Frankly, I have my doubts.

There is no doubt that some day I will do all of my weekend homework on Friday night instead of putting it off until bedtime on Sunday. When I do, I'll be able to relax and enjoy the whole weekend without any nagging feelings that I ought to be writing that report or reading those two chapters. I'll even be able to watch Sunday night television with a clear conscience.

Oh, it's going to be swell when some day comes. My dad's going to take golf lessons and get rid of his slice once and for all, and my mom's going to lose twenty pounds and not gain them back again. Our dog's going to go to one of those fancy grooming salons and get a decent haircut, instead of having us snip at him with the kitchen scissors.

We're going to have built-in bookshelves in the living room when some day comes and we're going to hire a cleaning service to wash all our windows, instead of doing them ourselves. Some day Grandma is going to knit sweaters and caps out of all those balls of yarn and some day I'll write the thank-you letters for my birthday presents the very next day.

Some day I'm going to leap out of bed the second my alarm clock rings. And some day I'll get my clothes and all my school things organized the night before so that I can get up and eat a leisurely breakfast and not feel rushed.

So many good things are going to happen some day.

I hope some day comes soon.

#44

The Dog Birthday Party

When my dog, B.J., and I were both ten years old, I decided to give him a birthday party. It seemed unfair that B.J. had lived for ten years and never had a birthday party. Of course, no one knew for sure when B.J.'s birthday was since the only papers he had were an adoption certificate from the Humane Society, stating that he was a stray, and the vaccination certificates from our vet, saying that B.J. received his shots each year.

Still, when we got him he was approximately six months old, so I figured out that his birthday was somewhere around the first of November. I declared November third as B.J.'s birthday, mainly because the third fell on a Saturday that year which would be a good day for a dog birthday party. I vowed to give B.J. a birthday he would never forget.

Since this was B.J.'s party, I decided the guests should be other dogs. Two of them, Jessie and Blue, were white poodles who belonged to Mrs. Levy, our next-door neighbor. B.J. saw them daily through the wire fence that separated our two back yards. He would run up and down on one side of the fence while Jessie and Blue galloped up and down on the other side. I knew B.J. would be thrilled to finally have Jessie and Blue on the same side of the fence with him, and I was sure Jessie and Blue would like it too.

I also invited my friends, Bill, Sharon and Dutch and told each of them to bring their dog. Dutch said his dog was duck hunting with his dad; he asked if he could bring Tiffany, his cat, instead. I said, "Why not?" B.J. didn't know any cats, but he was a friendly dog, so I thought he wouldn't mind if a cat attended his party.

I spent a long time planning the menu. I decided to serve dog biscuits, raw hamburger patties and V-8℠ juice. I included the V-8™ juice because that is one of B.J.'s favorite treats. He can smell it clear across the room. If anyone is drinking V-8™ juice, B.J. sits in front of them and whines and tries to look pathetic, as if he's about to die of malnutrition. When I have V-8™ juice, I always give him a spoonful in a saucer, but on his birthday, I decided to splurge and let B.J. and his guests have a whole can of V-8™ all to themselves. I poured it into saucers, with one saucer for each dog.

I didn't send out invitations. I just waited until November third. Then I called up Bill, Sharon and Dutch, told them what was up and asked them to bring their pets over. Mrs. Levy wasn't home, but Jessie and Blue were in the back yard so I opened the gate in the fence. Jessie and Blue came charging through.

B.J. went wild. He and Jessie began nipping each other, while Blue barked loudly and ran in circles.

B.J. and Jessie didn't fight, exactly. But they didn't sit cozily side by side, either. They wrestled and rolled and created such a loud ruckus that I didn't even hear Bill and Dutch arrive. I didn't know they were there until I heard Dutch scream.

Tiffany took one look at the party guests and climbed Dutch's arm. She was perched on his head, with her back arched and her claws imbedded in his scalp.

Meanwhile, Bill's dog, Fatso, ignored all the other dogs and went straight for the card table where I had the refreshments waiting. He stood on his hind legs and started gobbling the raw hamburger.

I yelled at Bill to make Fatso stop, but Bill was busy trying to get Tiffany's claws out of Dutch's head so that Dutch would quit screaming.

So I shouted at Fatso myself and clapped my hands loudly. When B.J. heard me holler, "No! No! Stop that!", he must have thought I was in danger because he quit biting Jessie's tail and headed for Fatso, with his neck fur bristling and his teeth bared.

Jessie and Blue followed him and when they saw Fatso eating the hamburger, they decided it was time for the refreshments.

Before I could stop them, they tried to climb up on the table and the table collapsed, spilling all the food on the ground. The little saucers of V-8™ juice all tipped, and the liquid sprayed all over Jessie's and Blue's white fur. The effect was startling. B.J. forgot about Fatso and began to lick Jessie instead.

By the time Sharon and Fluffie got there, the food was gone. Tiffany was gone, too, straight over the fence, and Dutch was threatening to sue me if he couldn't find her. Bill's face and arms were badly scratched from when he pried Tiffany off Dutch's head, and Fatso and Blue were fighting over who got to lick the plates. Sharon was furious because Fluffie missed the refreshments. She said it isn't polite to invite someone to a party and then not wait for them to arrive before you serve.

Before I could explain, Mrs. Levy got home. When she saw her formerly white dogs, she let out a scream like an Apache war cry. Even the dogs stopped fighting and turned to look at her. When she got done screaming, she demanded to know why I had opened the gate, stolen her dogs and allowed them to be mangled. She thought the V-8™ juice was blood. She even suggested that B.J. was a cannibal dog who was trying to eat Jessie.

Eventually I got everyone calmed down, but it wiped out my savings account. I had to pay for Dutch and Bill to go to the doctor because the cat scratches on their arms got infected. I paid the poodle parlor to shampoo Jessie and Blue. It required a special rinse to get the pink tinge out of their fur. I put a LOST ad in the newspaper, but before the ad appeared, Tiffany found her own way home, none the worse for her adventure. I even had a veterinary bill because Fatso not only ate all the raw hamburger, he also ate part of one of the broken saucers and it had to be removed surgically from his large intestine.

In spite of everything, I did accomplish my goal. It was definitely a birthday that B.J. — and I — will never forget.

#45

Read Any Good
Dictionaries Lately?

I've discovered the dictionary. Not for looking up what words mean. I've looked up meanings in the dictionary ever since I was in first grade. Now I've discovered the dictionary is fun to read. It's full of information that I'd never find anywhere else.

For example, I learned from the dictionary that cereal leaf beetles are small, reddish brown beetles with black heads. They feed on cereal grasses and are a serious threat to grain crops in the United States. Imagine! My Wheaties™ and corn flakes are in dire danger from cereal leaf beetles and I didn't even know it.

Another thing I learned by reading the dictionary is that a sidereal hour is the twenty-fourth part of a sidereal day and a sidereal minute is the sixtieth part of a sidereal hour. It's hard to work this knowledge into an ordinary conversation, but if sidereal time is ever mentioned, I'll be ready.

I've found that it's best to read the dictionary a small portion at a time. That way I retain what I read. If I read several pages at a time, the words pass through my brain as if they were written in pencil and immediately erased. When I read just one or two definitions at a time, they stay, like indelible ink.

Before I started reading the dictionary for pleasure, I didn't know that an octopus always has eight arms. Now I know. I also know that an octameter is a line of verse which has eight metrical feet and an octapeptide is a protein fragment which consists of eight amino acids. An octet is a musical composition for eight instruments or eight voices, while an octandrious flower is one with eight stamens. I thought I'd caught on to all the *octo* words until I came to October. It's the tenth month in our year, not the eighth.

One of my all-time favorite words is *incorporeal*. It is an adjective which means having no material body or form.

Incorporeity is the quality or state of being incorporeal. If you are an incorporeity, you are a ghost. Ghost is a rather plain word, I think. Straight forward. Simple.

But incorporeity rolls deliciously off my tongue and hints of haunted houses. Next Halloween I intend to dress up as an incorporeity.

Not all of the new words I've learned are long or difficult to remember. For example, there is ta. It's spelled T, A. Ta. According to my dictionary, ta is British baby talk which means "thanks". I wonder if all the babies in England say, "ta" when someone changes their diapers. When they're older and get birthday presents from their relatives, they probably write ta letters.

I rather like the word, ta. Thank you seems too stiff and formal. Thanks has such a nasal ring to it. But ta is just right and I intend to use it from now on.

I knew what gutters on a house were, even before I read the definition. I knew what gutter language was too. But I didn't know that a candle can gutter out. It gets gradually weaker and finally quits burning. A person's career can gutter out, too, by ending feebly — dwindling away to nothing.

Because I do not want this speech to gutter out, I will quit now, even though I have a few sidereal seconds left. If you read anything good in the dictionary, let me know.

Ta.

#46

Things I Wish I Had Not Said

If I could learn to keep my mouth shut, my life would be less complicated. I have a knack for either saying the right thing at the wrong time, or the wrong thing at the right time. Sometimes it's the wrong thing at the wrong time.

Like the time I should have been quiet at Uncle Irwin's wedding.

My mother calls Uncle Irwin the black sheep of the family and tolerates him only because he is my father's brother. Uncle Irwin is my favorite relative. He used to show up periodically and stay a few days. Then he'd leave again and we wouldn't hear from him for months and months.

While he was with us, he showed me card tricks and taught me riddles. He came to my school's football game once, even though I only sat on the bench.

At the end of each visit, he always gave me a five dollar bill. He would fold it up small and hold it in his palm and then, when he said goodbye, he'd shake my hand and slip me the money. He always winked and I knew I wasn't supposed to tell anyone. It was for me to spend on anything I wanted — gummie bears or baseball cards or hot fudge sundaes — with nobody to suggest I save part of it.

Once I asked Uncle Irwin where he got all his money and he told me he didn't have any. He said he borrowed from my dad, but he would pay it all back some day.

When Uncle Irwin got married, we went to the wedding. While we waited for the service to begin, Mother said she was curious to know what sort of woman would choose to spend her life with Uncle Irwin.

And *I* said, "Maybe she's rich and now he will be able to repay all the money he borrowed from Dad."

As soon as I said it, I knew it was a mistake. Dad glared at me and Mom glared at Dad. When they got home, they had a rousing fight. It seems my mother didn't know anything about the loans to Uncle Irwin and she was none too happy to find out.

I also should have kept my mouth shut when our next-door neighbors, the Crumpets, had their house for sale. I was outside riding my bike when some people came to look at the Crumpet's house. They stayed a long time and then they walked all around the yard. There was a girl about my age with them, and after awhile she got tired of looking at the roof and came over to talk to me. She told me her parents might buy the Crumpet's house. She also told me she had a big white dog.

I thought it would be great to have a kid my age next door, especially one with a dog. I'd always wanted a dog, but all I ever had was goldfish. I decided to tell the girl all the good things I could think of about the Crumpet's house. She could tell her parents and maybe they would decide to buy it.

First I told her how the basement floods each spring and she could sail boats down there. Our basement floods too, but not as much as the Crumpet's. I've always wanted to sail my boats in their basement. I said maybe we could even have boat races.

Next I told her how all the kids in the area play kick-the-can during the summer. We always play on our block because the hedges and trees make good hiding places. The games usually go on long after it gets dark, and since the street light is in front of the Crumpet's house, that's always home base. I told her she'd never miss any of the fun; she couldn't help but hear us, right in front of her house.

I also told her there's a fire station just around the corner and we can hear the fire sirens go off. "It's exciting at night," I said. "The sirens wake you up and you can watch out the window and see the engines go by."

The more I talked, the more I could tell she really liked the idea of living in the Crumpet's house. I was sure I'd helped Mr.

Crumpet make the sale. I could hardly wait for the new people and their dog to move in.

The next day Mr. Crumpet came over. I thought he was going to thank me or maybe even offer me a reward for my help. Sort of like a sales commission.

He didn't offer a reward. He didn't thank me, either. He was furious. He told my parents that his house had been sold, but the buyers changed their minds after I told them the house has a drainage problem and the neighborhood is too noisy.

I protested that I was only trying to help, but he didn't believe me. I was forbidden to talk to any other prospective buyers.

The people who eventually bought the house are crabby and have no pets. They don't even have any kids. They complained so much about our kick-the-can games that we finally had to move one block over to play, where the hiding places aren't as good.

If any other house is put up for sale, I won't say a word to any prospective buyers. I won't even mention how the electricity in this area goes off all the time in the winter, and we get to eat by candlelight and not do our homework. The buyers will just have to discover the good things for themselves.

#47

Big Black Lies

When adults fail to tell the truth, the failure is usually called a "little white lie." But when kids fail to tell the truth, it's not only a Big Black Lie, it's practically the end of the world.

For example, the other night Mom and Dad made a big bowl of buttered popcorn and turned on their favorite TV show. Just as the opening music started, Mrs. Schnotzer called and asked Mom and Dad to fill in at the Schnotzer's bridge club. One of the regular couples couldn't make it at the last minute.

Mom told Mrs. Schnotzer that she was terribly sorry, but Dad wasn't feeling well. She said he was lying down. Dad promptly lay down on the sofa, with one hand in the popcorn bowl and the other hand giving Mom the thumb's up sign.

After Mom hung up, I accused her of not telling the truth. She said it was just a little white lie, a way to keep from hurting Mrs. Schnotzer's feelings. She couldn't very well tell Mrs. Schnotzer that she and Dad would rather stay home and watch TV than to play bridge with her, so she was forced to tell a little white lie.

A few days later, my history teacher told my class to turn in our written reports on the U.S. Congress. All around me the other kids opened notebooks and folders. They removed neatly written pages about the Congress. The teacher started down the aisle, collecting the reports.

My mouth felt dry. How could it be Friday already? What had happened to Thursday night, the night I promised myself I would do my report?

Oh, yes. On Thursday night, a bunch of neighborhood kids got up a softball game and we played until it was too dark to see the ball. When I got home from softball, my Uncle Bruce and Aunt Sue were at our house, and Aunt Sue had brought one of her pecan pies. Aunt Sue's pecan pies have won three Blue Ribbons in the Community Club's annual Favorite Recipe Contest. Who can think about the U.S. Congress when there's a piece of pecan pie a la mode staring you in the face?

My teacher stopped beside my desk and looked at me expectantly. "Do you have your report?" she asked.

I shook my head.

Why couldn't she just leave it at that? She asked if I had my report; I told her, "no." Why couldn't she just give me an *F* and go on to the next desk? But no. She had to ask me why I didn't have it.

I couldn't tell her I didn't have it because I was more interested in playing softball and eating Aunt Sue's pecan pie than I was in the U.S. Congress. So I said I didn't do my report because when I got home from school yesterday there was an ambulance in our driveway with its red light whirling.

I was so shocked when I saw it that I dropped my homework on the grass, and ran into my house to see what was wrong. I said I got there just as they were wheeling my Dad out of the kitchen. His face was white and he told me he had terrible chest pains. He thought it was his heart.

Our neighbor came over and offered to drive me to the hospital. I called Mom at work and she said she'd meet me there.

It was only a mild heart attack, thank goodness, but it was after midnight before we got back home. I was exhausted, but I took a flashlight out on the lawn to look for my school work. When Mom asked me what on earth I was doing, I told her I had to write a report on the Congress and I had dropped my research notes. She said, "Never mind the report, your teacher will understand if it's late."

My teacher did understand. She patted my shoulder and said she hoped my father was feeling better and that I could have three extra days to turn in my report.

We were finishing our dinner that night when the telephone rang. Dad answered. First he looked surprised. Then he looked angry. Then he hung up the phone and started yelling at me.

I tried to explain that I had only told a little white lie. I said it was necessary to avoid hurting my teacher's feelings. But nobody would listen.

#48

I Used to Think

For the first ten years of my life, I had dozens of misconceptions about the world. Most happened because I did not understand what I was told. I *thought* I understood, so I never asked questions. I just went about believing things which were not true.

For example, I could never figure out why Joseph and Mary filled the manger with peas. Peas are not my favorite vegetable; they are a poor fourth to corn, beans and carrots. I certainly would not want to sleep in a mess of squishy, green peas, no matter how heavenly they might be. Yet every Christmas, for many years, I sang it out, loud and clear: "Sleep in heavenly pea . .eas; sle-eep in heavenly peas." As I sang, I had a vivid mental image. I always wondered how they got the green stains out of the swaddling clothes.

I had vivid mental images for another song, too. We have always called the electric stove in our kitchen a "range" and when I went to kindergarten, I learned a marvelous song in which deer and antelope played on top of our kitchen stove. Buffalo lived there too, and we all roamed happily around the kitchen together. I did wonder how any cooking got done, but the idea of all those exotic animals living in our kitchen and jumping up on our range was exciting.

For years I refused to eat poppy seed rolls. The first time I was told what they were, I heard "puppy" seed rolls, and I thought if those puppy seeds were planted instead of eaten, they might grow into baby dogs. It seemed cruel to waste the puppy seeds by sprinkling them on hamburger buns, and I was not about to eat them.

I also thought that pasteurized milk was milk which had somehow been blessed by the pastor of a church before it left the dairy. I assumed it was the protestant equivalent of holy water.

My grandmother used to complain that she had "gas in her stomach ." This fascinated me, and I wished I could go with her sometime when she went to the gas station to get a refill. Until I heard Grandma talk about gas in her stomach, I wondered what belly buttons were for. Then I figured out that this was where the gas goes in.

Personally, I never wanted to pour gasoline in *my* belly button, but Grandma put a lot of strange things in her stomach. She regularly swallowed antacid tablets, which I thought were some sort of pesticide, much like what my mother sprayed along the baseboard when the ants got in our cupboard.

I barely knew how to print my name when my older brother informed me that his class was learning cursive writing. I was shocked. I couldn't believe that his teacher would give the entire class instructions on how to write swear words. Secretly, I hoped my brother would get in big trouble with our parents when he showed them what he was learning.

Looking back on it now, I can understand why a little kid might get mixed up by antacid tablets and heavenly peace. But I even got the fairy tales wrong. I always wondered what *idge* tasted like. I'd eaten poor boy sandwiches, but never poor idge. The three bears complained bitterly when Goldilocks ate their poor idge so it must be good, but we never had idge for dinner and I was always curious about it.

I was curious about many things, such as where tow truck drivers got enough toes, and who they delivered the toes to. I wondered why there didn't seem to be any finger trucks.

I can laugh at myself as I look back at all of this, but it makes me nervous, too. I wonder how much of what I think *now* is true and how much is one more misconception.

#49

Don't Believe a Word I Say

Before I give my speech, I have to tell you what happened to me just now, right outside the door. I know I'm supposed to do my monolog, but this won't take long, and I think it might be important. After I tell you what happened, you may want to call the police or something, and I don't think we should wait while I go all the way through the piece I've memorized. A couple of minutes could make a big difference.

While I was sitting out there, practicing my speech and waiting for my turn, a woman came up to me. She was nicely dressed, and I thought she was *(Use appropriate term, such as a teacher or the director)*. She said, "Hello," and I said, "Hello," and she asked me my name and I told her and then her eyes got all big and round, and she gasped for breath and she stared at me, as if I'd said I was some famous person.

She asked me how old I am and I told her, and then she asked me when I was born and I told her, and she kept looking astonished, as if she couldn't believe what I said.

And then, do you know what she said to me? Out of the clear blue, this lady I'd never seen before in my life, got tears in her eyes and she said, "I know this will be a shock to you, but I am your mother."

I stared at her. I began to wonder if this was some wacko person and we should be calling the psychiatric ward. But she didn't *seem* crazy; she seemed well educated and proper and, well, nice — the sort of ladies my mom has for friends.

I told her she must be mistaken because I already have a mother and she said, of course I was referring to my adoptive mother, but that she was my birth mother and she'd been searching for me for years. She said it was a private adoption and she didn't know anything about the adoptive parents, but that she had signed the papers only on condition that she could choose the baby's name. She said I am named after her father *(Mother)*.

Now, it was news to me that I was adopted, but naturally I started to wonder if maybe my folks had kept it a secret from me. This person seemed so sure, and she did have hair the same color as mine.

I asked her what made her think I was her kid before she found out my name and my birthday, and she said the minute she saw me, she knew. That's why she came over to talk to me. She said I am the spitting image of my father, and that once I saw a picture of him, there would be no doubt in my mind. I asked her to show me the picture and she said she doesn't carry one with her, but that she has an old one at her house, and if I would go home with her, she'd be glad to show it to me and also to show me the official birth certificate which would prove when and where I was born.

It made me feel really strange, listening to her tell me that she's my birth mother. It would be a weird feeling even if I had always known I was adopted, but it's really weird when I never suspected that somewhere in the world there might be a woman who was searching for me because she was my birth mother.

I told her I'd like to see some proof, but that I couldn't go home with her now because it was almost my turn to do my monolog. I said as soon as I was finished, I'd go with her.

When I said that, she got angry and said she couldn't wait. She said wasn't it more important to find out about my birth parents than it was to do a monolog? She said she was offering me information that could change my entire life, and if I had any sense, I'd walk right out of here and go with her.

I almost did it. I got up and started to follow her to her car, and then I remembered my mom and dad telling me not ever to go anywhere with a stranger, no matter what kind of story the person told me. So I said I had to come in here first and tell the *(Director? Teacher?)* that I wouldn't be doing my piece and then I'd be right back out, but instead I really came to tell you about the woman and to see if you think I should call my folks and ask them if I'm really adopted or if we should call the police, or . . . .

Oh. I see my time is up. Before I sit down, I probably should tell you that there really wasn't any woman outside; I just wanted to have your full attention.

#50

Never Sleep in Your Underwear

My family takes turns doing the chores. One week I do the dinner dishes, one week I vacuum and dust, and one week I do the laundry. The week of the big flood, it was my turn to do the laundry. Unfortunately, I hadn't yet done it when disaster hit.

I intended to do it Friday night. The house rule is that laundry MUST be done no later than noon on Saturday, or the person whose job it is can not go anywhere Saturday afternoon or evening. Of course, I *could* have done the laundry on Tuesday, Wednesday or Thursday, but I had a lot of homework on Tuesday, and there was good TV on Wednesday, and on Thursday I just didn't feel like it.

After school on Friday, my aunt and uncle called and invited me to go out for a hamburger and to a movie with them. Their treat. I couldn't pass up a deal like that. I decided to get up early Saturday morning, even though it's my only day to sleep in, and do the laundry then.

When I got home from the movie, I put on my pajamas and carried a glass of milk and a bag of cookies to the kitchen table. The cookie bag wouldn't open. I tugged and pulled. Finally I grabbed it in both hands and jerked as hard as I could — and knocked the glass of milk right into my lap. My other pajamas were in the pile of dirty laundry.

And that's how I happened to be sleeping in my underwear the night the water main burst. I woke up when my dad yelled at me. I could hear a loud, rumbling noise and I wondered if a truck had somehow driven into our living room.

"Get up!" Dad yelled. "Get out of the house. Fast!"

My eyes flew open and I realized the noise wasn't a truck. It was water. Water was gushing into our house!

I sat up and swung my feet over the side of the bed —

into what felt like a river. Water swirled around my ankles and I could tell it was rising fast.

There was no time to grab a bathrobe. There was no time to do anything but scramble out of bed, and wade through the icy water.

My parents and my sister were right ahead of me. The water moved so fast that it was hard to walk, so we all held hands to make sure nobody slipped.

It wasn't much better outside. The water main had burst directly opposite our house, so all the water was pouring straight at our front door. The force of it had pushed the door open, even though the door was locked.

A police officer waded toward us and we struggled up the street, still holding hands. Lights were going on all over the neighborhood, and police cars and fire engines were already there.

So was a TV news crew, complete with lights and cameras. They filmed us as we sloshed out of our house and made our way uphill. We stood above the broken main and watched the water gush toward our front door.

City crews quickly turned off the main water supply. The pipe was repaired the next day, and the insurance company paid to get our house repainted and for new carpets and furniture.

It all turned out OK, according to my parents. Nobody was hurt and they like the new furniture.

It wasn't OK with me, though. There was one huge problem: all my friends saw me on TV, wearing nothing but my underwear. It was terrible! My mom and dad and sister all had on pajamas, but not me. I had to appear before the whole world in my underwear. When I complained to Mom, she asked me why I hadn't worn my pajamas and I said both pairs were dirty, and she said since it was my week to do laundry, I had no one to blame but myself, and she hopes I learned a lesson.

I sure did. I learned never to sleep in my underwear.

#51

Pulling Rank

My parents like to pretend that our family system is a democracy, but it isn't. It's a dictatorship, with two dictators. Anytime there's a disagreement, my parents pull rank.

For example, if I happen to get the evening paper first, and my dad comes home from work and wants to read the sports page or the business section, I'm expected to give it to him. And if I point out that I had the paper first and shouldn't have to give it up until I'm finished, he says he's had a hard day at work and he wants to relax with the newspaper, and not to give him any flak.

Once my friend, P.J., was at my house and we were sitting in the living room listening to records and Pastor Lindquest from our church stopped by. Mom made P.J. and me leave so that she and Pastor Lindquest could sit in the living room.

Mom told us to go upstairs and listen to records in my bedroom. I didn't see why P.J. and I should be the ones to leave. We had the living room first; why couldn't Mom take Pastor Lindquest into *her* bedroom if they wanted to talk? I suggested that, but Mom's face turned red, and she told me and P.J. to *Move it. Right now!*

When Mom says *Move it* in that tone of voice, I know better than to hang around and argue. Still, I don't think people should pull rank on other people. Just because my parents are older and bigger than I am, they act like I don't have any rights.

My little brother, Gary, doesn't have any rights, either. Dad made Gary take down a complete haunted house that Gary had built in the garage, just because Dad wanted to put his new car inside, out of the snow. Gary cried and said it took him six hours to put up the haunted house — he even had cold spaghetti hanging from the rafter, like worms. Dad said that was too bad, but

Gary should have built the haunted house in his own room, not the garage.

Gary said when he grows up he won't be such a mean father. He said if he ever has a little kid who wants to build a haunted house in the garage, he'll let him keep it there for weeks and weeks. Dad said he hopes when Gary grows up he can afford to buy a new car once every six years and that he won't have to keep it outside in the snow.

My parents are especially ready to pull rank when it comes to chores. One day last summer, we were all supposed to work in the garden. The weeds were choking out the green beans and the corn was as thirsty as a dog who's been to the vet. Gary and I didn't want to pull weeds or water the corn, so we said we'd pick blackberries instead, from the wild blackberry vines that grow in the empty lot just down the street. Mom said if we'd pick the berries, she'd bake us a blackberry pie for dinner.

Gary and I took empty coffee cans to put the blackberries in. On our way to the empty lot, we put a few stones in the coffee cans and tried to see how much racket we could make while we walked along. With each step we took, we shook the cans and listened to the stones rattle.

The berries were fat and juicy and we picked the plumpest ones and dropped them into our coffee cans. Without thinking, I gave my can a shake, the way I'd been doing as we walked along. The stones were still in it, and when I shook the stones and those ripe blackberries together, there wasn't much left of the berries.

"Look," I said to Gary. "Blackberry ink." He peered into my coffee can, grinned, and quickly shook some berries and stones together in *his* coffee can. We put our hands over the open ends of the cans and whirled those stones and berries around like sixty. I wished we had a jiggle machine like they have in the paint store, to really shake things up, but even without a jiggle machine, we did a dandy job of liquifying those blackberries. It was the finest blackberry ink ever created.

We found little sticks to use as pens. We dipped the sticks

into the blackberry ink and wrote our names on our arms. Then we made designs on our khaki pants. Gary made blackberry ink flags, complete with fifty stars. I made blackberry ink elephants — six of them, all in a row, marching trunk-to-tail down my left pant leg.

We were sitting in the dirt, finishing the pictures on our pants, when Mom came over to see why it was taking so long for us to pick enough blackberries for a pie.

For the rest of the afternoon, Gary and I had to pull weeds. Mom and Dad sat in the shade and drank iced tea and watched us. Talk about pulling rank! And when we were done weeding, we had to scrub our pants with bleach. It didn't help, though. The flags and elephants were there to stay.

I've thought about organizing a protest. If Gary and I banded together and demanded our rights, maybe we'd get some action. The trouble is, I think I know what sort of action we'd get. Some parents are determined to pull rank, no matter how unfair it might be.

#52

Letters to Grandpa

I write to my grandpa every week. My mom writes to him too. He never reads our letters.

Grandpa lives in a nursing home. He has Alzheimer's disease and it's destroying his brain.

It's been years since Grandpa was able to read or to understand what is read to him. We usually send him greeting cards or postcards with bright, cheerful pictures. When my grandma visits him, she holds the cards up to show him the pictures, but he doesn't look at them.

I can hear Grandma's happy voice as she holds my latest card in front of him. "Look, Honey," she'll say. "You got a letter from *(Name)*. They picked apples and wish you could be there to eat applesauce with them."

He doesn't understand. He doesn't remember me. He doesn't even remember Mom and she's his only daughter.

Grandpa has been in the nursing home for six years. He is fed, bathed, dressed and undressed, wheeled outside for some fresh air. He does not speak or react when he's spoken to. He stares, and drools, and dozes.

Six years is a long, long time. Six years ago, I was only in (_____) grade.

My friend, Claire, asked why we bother to spend money on cards and postage when Grandpa doesn't know the difference.

It's true. He doesn't know the difference.

Mom says there are thousands of forgotten people in nursing homes, people who never have visitors, and never get any mail. She says that will not happen to *her* father. Our family doesn't forget.

When I was little, Grandpa used to play cards with me. He took me swimming, too, and then we'd dry off and sit in the sun together and talk. Before I could read, he read books to me, and after I learned to read, he let me read books to him.

When the nurse's aide distributes the mail, she talks to Grandpa. She says, "Hello. There's a letter for you today." For a moment, she sees him not as just another patient with blank eyes, but as a man who is loved. Someone, somewhere, loves him enough to write to him. She smiles at him and pats his hand.

When Grandma visits him, she tapes his cards to the wall opposite his bed. They hang there — the pictures of red geraniums and fuzzy brown puppies and yellow hot air balloons — a rainbow of messages, mailed one at a time. They say: *We're thinking of you. We love you.*

Grandpa doesn't notice. He doesn't know the cards are from me and Mom. We are nine hundred miles away and he can't remember us. We remember him though.

I write to my grandpa every week. He doesn't know I do it.

But I know.

#53

Trading in Old Turtle

For as long as I could remember, our family car was a beat-up old green station wagon. We called it turtle because it didn't have any oomph when it went uphill. Mom always complained because Turtle sputtered and choked when it started and Dad said Turtle had never heard of fuel economy.

There was a dent in the front fender from the time someone ran into Turtle while we were in the movies. Whoever it was didn't even leave a note on our windshield, and we all agreed it was a rotten thing to do. We never got the dent fixed because our insurance was five-hundred dollars deductible and it was going to cost four-hundred and seventy-five dollars to fix the dent, and my parents said Turtle wasn't worth it. Still, we got angry every time we looked at the dent.

One of Turtle's back windows never worked right. If you rolled it too far, it stuck and wouldn't roll back up again. My little brother, Joey, was always rolling it too far and then we'd have to stop the car and Dad would get out his screwdriver and fix the window, and tell Joey, again, not to roll the window all the way down. Once Joey did it when it was raining and Dad was so mad, he refused to stop and fix it and the rain blew in on Joey all the way home.

When my mom got a raise, she and Dad sat at the kitchen table, figuring out their budget, and then they said we were going to shop for a new car.

Every Saturday for a month, we went to different car lots and looked at all the new kinds of cars. Sometimes we took them out for a test drive. It was great! Joey and I sat in the back seat. I reported on the leg room and Joey found out how well the windows worked.

Mom and Dad read about cars in the consumer magazines

and asked all of their friends what they liked and didn't like about their cars.

Finally, the decision was made. The new car was white, with bucket seats. It even had automatic windows, which cost extra. Dad looked hard at Joey and said it would be worth it.

When the day came to pick up the new car, we were too excited to eat breakfast. We drove Turtle to the car lot; we were trading her in as part of the down payment. Joey and I waited in Turtle while Mom and Dad went in to sign the final papers and get the keys.

Joey rolled the window down to get some fresh air. He rolled it too far and it stuck. I asked him if he remembered the time he rolled it too far when it was raining, and he asked if I remembered the time we took all my friends to the park for my birthday party, and Mom put the cake on Turtle's roof while we got in, and then she drove off and we saw the cake go sailing past the window. Then we started laughing and talking about all the funny things that had happened in Turtle.

There was the camping trip when the tent leaked and Joey and I had to sleep in Turtle. There was the time the Cub Scouts went on a field trip to the weather station and one of the drivers didn't show up, so everyone piled into Turtle, sitting on top of each other and punching and wiggling.

Joey stopped laughing and looked at me. "I'm going to miss old Turtle," he said. His chin was quivering and there were tears in his eyes.

I realized *I* was going to miss Turtle, too. I said, "What if someone buys her who is mean to her? What if *no one* buys her and she is hauled to one of those junk yards for old cars and allowed to get all rusty? What if she's put in a compactor and squeezed flat?"

Joey was bawling by then, and I started to cry, too. When our parents returned and heard what was wrong with us, Mom burst into tears. She said she had brought both of her babies home from the hospital in Turtle.

Dad looked at Mom. He looked at Joey and at me. He said he had just agreed to spend an incredible amount of money for a new car and now none of us wanted it.

Mom wiped her eyes and told him we did want the new car, but it was hard to leave Turtle, all the same. Then she told us to get out and to go get in the new car. She said a nice young couple with a baby was waiting to look at Turtle as soon as the dealer gave Turtle a tune-up. I don't know if Mom was telling the truth or not, but it made Joey and me feel better to think of some other kid growing up and riding around in Turtle.

We all piled into the new car and talked about how different it smelled inside. On the way home, Joey put his window up and down six times and it never stuck once. When we zipped right up a hill, we decided to name the new car Peter, after Peter Rabbit. At home, the neighbors came out to see our new car, and Mom let Joey and me each invite a friend over to go for a ride.

Once, many months later, I thought I saw Turtle chugging down the street. I couldn't be sure because there wasn't any dent in the fender, but I figured her new owners probably had the dent fixed. I was glad about that. I wonder if they had the window fixed too. I wouldn't trade Peter now for anything, but I'll never forget Turtle and all the fun we had together.

#54

The Doggie Dictionary

I am here as a public service to dog owners. Many dog owners are not aware of the existence of the International Doggie Dictionary. The definitions in this Doggie Dictionary are ancient truths, passed from generation to generation of dogs as part of the folklore of canines.

All puppies are taught these definitions by their mothers. Say a word from the Doggie Dictionary and all dogs know exactly what it means. Unfortunately, many humans who *think* they know the meaning of these words, don't realize that dogs interpret them differently.

In an attempt to reduce misunderstandings between dogs and their owners, I will share with you some of the proper definitions from the Doggie Dictionary.

LEASH.   A leash is a strap which attaches to your collar, enabling you to lead your owner where you want to go when you're out for a walk.

DOG BED.   This is any soft, clean surface, such as the white bedspread in the guest room, or the newly upholstered chair in the living room.

DROOL.   Drool is what you do when your owner has food and you don't. To drool properly, you must sit as close as possible, look sadly at your owner, and let your mouth hang open. Allow the saliva to drip into a pool on the floor.

SNIFF.   Sniffing is a social custom to use when you greet other dogs. Place your nose as close as possible to the other dog's rear end, and inhale deeply. Repeat several times, or until your owner makes you stop.

GARBAGE CAN.   A garbage can is a container which your neighbors put out once a week to test your ingenuity. You must stand on your hind feet and try to push the lid off with your nose.

If you practice diligently, you will be rewarded by the opportunity to shred margarine wrappers, gnaw on beef bones, and consume moldy bread crusts.

BICYCLES.   Bicycles are two-wheeled exercise machines, invented to give dogs a way to control body fat and help their hearts and lungs. For maximum aerobic benefit, you should hide in the bushes near a road and wait until the bicycle is six feet away. Then dash out, bark loudly, and run alongside it for several yards. If the person on the bicycle swerves, return to the bushes.

GUESTS.   Guests are people who come to your home to see you whine at the table, bark loudly, jump up on women wearing pantyhose, and do other tricks which you wouldn't think of doing just for the family. If the guests put their coats on your owner's bed, it means they want you to sleep there.

DEAFNESS.   This is a malady which affects dogs whose owners want them to come in when they want to stay out. Symptoms include staring blankly at the owner, running in the opposite direction, or lying down.

THUNDER.   Thunder is a signal that the end of the world is imminent. Owners remain amazingly calm during thunderstorms, so it is necessary for you to warn them of the danger by trembling uncontrollably, panting, rolling your eyes wildly, and following at their heels. If your owner should try to calm you during a thunderstorm, refuse to be comforted. Continue to shake.

WASTEBASKET.   This is a dog toy, usually round, which contains discarded tissues, candy wrappers, envelopes and other chewable items. When you get bored because you've been left alone, tip over the wastebasket and strew the contents around the house. It will keep you occupied until your owner returns.

FENCE.   A game of skill, the object of which is to get on the other side as quickly as possible. You may be able to go over the top; usually it's faster to dig underneath.

DOOR.   A door is a rectangle to scratch on when your feet are muddy, so that your owner will let you in. If your feet are not muddy, don't scratch; the weather is too nice to go inside.

SOFA.   Sofas are to dogs what napkins are to people. After eating, it is polite to run up and down the front of the sofa and wipe your whiskers clean.

BATH.   A bath is a process used by dog owners for drenching the floors, walls, and themselves with water. You can help by shaking vigorously and frequently.

LOVE.   All dogs know this last definition, even before their mothers tell them. Love is a feeling of intense affection, given freely and with no restrictions. The best way to show your love is to wag your tail. If you're lucky, a person will love you in return.

#55

Toasting Marshmallows on the Right Front Burner

Mom used to nag me to learn to cook. She said if I knew how to cook, I would never again have to complain because I don't like what we're having for dinner.

Several times she showed me easy recipes in her cookbooks and suggested that I try making them, but I was never in the mood.

Then one day I got home from school early and I finished all my homework and none of my friends were around to talk to on the phone. I decided to surprise Mom and cook something.

First I paged through one of the cookbooks, but the recipes that sounded good were too complicated. They all required sifting flour or melting butter or chopping nuts. I wanted something easy, fast and yummy. Like the stuff we used to make at camp.

Thinking of camp made me remember my favorite dessert in the whole world: schmores. I suppose every kid has made schmores at some time or other. The first time I had them, I was at scout camp and later our whole sixth grade class made them when we went on an end-of-the-year picnic.

Schmores are easy to make. You roast a marshmallow, place it on a graham cracker, smash it down with part of a chocolate bar and put another graham cracker on top.

I looked in the cupboard. We had a box of graham crackers and a bag of marshmallows. We even had one chocolate bar. All I needed was the campfire.

It was February. In Minnesota. An outdoor fire was out of the question, and we don't have a fireplace in our house.

So I did the only sensible thing. I turned the right front burner of the electric stove to "HIGH", and waited until it was bright red. Then I stuck a marshmallow on a dinner fork and held it over the burner.

I turned it around and around, watching the outside get puffy and golden. Timing is important when you make schmores. If you don't toast the marshmallow long enough, the inside won't squish when you press the chocolate into it. If you toast it too long, of course, the marshmallow burns.

The perfect moment is when the outside of the marshmallow is crispy brown and the inside is so smooth and gooey that the marshmallow droops downward from the fork. By rotating it quickly, gravity works to keep the marshmallow from falling off while you whisk it away from the fire and onto your graham cracker.

I waited a split second too long. Before I could whisk it onto the graham cracker, the marshmallow fell off the fork onto the hot burner.

When you drop a marshmallow into a campfire, you just let it burn up. It's kind of fun to watch it sizzle and turn black and crumble into ashes. It wasn't fun when the marshmallow was sizzling on the right front burner of Mom's electric stove.

For one thing, it was not a pleasant smell. Also, the smoke alarm went off and I couldn't figure out how to disconnect it. It was still shrieking when Mom came home, which may be just as well, since it made it impossible for me to hear what she said.

I never did get my schmores that day. Mom says I'll have to wait until the weather's nice enough to have a campfire.

One good thing did come of this: Mom no longer nags me to cook dinner.

#56

Boom Butts in the Bean Patch

As an amateur photographer, I always dreamed of taking a picture that has universal appeal — the kind that gets picked up by the Associated Press or reprinted in *Life* magazine. I took such a picture last summer. It's the best photo I ever shot and I titled it, "Boom Butts in the Bean Patch."

My grandpa has a huge vegetable garden and in the summer, all my relatives visit him because they want to take home a bag of Grandpa's sweet corn, or green beans or huge, juicy tomatoes.

The relatives must pick their own produce. Grandpa says he does the planting, watering and weeding, so folks can do the harvesting themselves.

Grandpa plants bush beans, and over the years, I have observed two main methods which people use to pick them. Kids under ten years old, squat. They just hunker down on their haunches in between rows of beans. When the bushes next to them have been picked clean, they waddle, duck-fashion, to the next bush.

Adults bend at the waist, letting their arms dangle forward into the bean bushes. This method is easier on the legs than squatting. It also gives anyone standing behind them a wide-angle view of the bean picker's rear end. Even slim people with narrow hips look broad in the beam when they're viewed from behind as they bend over to pick beans.

My relatives are not slim people with narrow hips. They are sturdy people with — well, if I wanted to be polite here, I would say broad hips. To be honest, I will say that our family has long lamented the hereditary tendency of what we call "boom butt." Anyone unlucky enough to have the family boom butt does not fit in size eight jeans. No amount of dieting or exercising decreases the girth of those afflicted with boom butt. After awhile, they give up trying to change their shapes. They relax, accept themselves as they are, and enjoy life. "Enjoy life" means, since the bone structure of their hips prevents them from ever looking slim, they may as well eat, drink, and have another piece of chocolate cream pie. Why fight destiny?

I'm telling you all of this background so that you will be able to appreciate what a sight it is when my relatives gather to pick beans. On the most memorable occasion, there were six of them — three aunts, two uncles and my mother, all at various places along the rows of beans, all bent at the waist with their rears to the sky. If I'd had a pea shooter, I don't think I could have controlled myself.

I didn't have a pea shooter; I did have a camera. The picture is a little shaky because I was laughing so hard, but that photo is still a sight to behold. It definitely has universal appeal.

When I first got the picture back from the developer, I took it to my mother. I told her if it's true that laughter heals the sick, I should sell enlargements of my picture to hospitals and clinics. They'd be able to discharge their patients twice as fast.

When I showed her the photo, she didn't laugh. She didn't even smile. She said the picture is disgusting and accused me of purposefully choosing an angle which made her look wider than she is. I started to say I didn't *have* to choose a special angle, that *any* angle had the same effect, but I could tell from the look in her eye that I'd better keep quiet.

When I showed "Boom Butts in the Bean Patch" to the aunts and uncles in the picture, they didn't laugh either. Two of them threatened dire consequences if any eyes other than our immediate family should see it.

What a loss for the Associated Press and *Life* magazine.

#57

Getting to the Point, the Long Way

Some people cannot say anything without digressing. Ask such a person a straightforward question, such as "Did it rain last night?" and you will never get a yes-or-no answer. Instead, you will hear about the television program that was on last night, including the commercials. You will hear about K-Mart's sale on umbrellas. You will learn that Mrs. Simpson's roof is leaking and the estimate for a new roof was more than five-thousand dollars, which Mrs. Simpson cannot afford. What you will *not* learn is whether or not it rained last night.

My friend, Jason, is such a person. Jason loves verbal detours. He thinks the only way to go from Point A to Point B is via Points O, P, and Q.

Jason called me last night and said, "Guess what I found on the way home from school."

I couldn't guess. It turned out that Jason found a dollar on the sidewalk. But did Jason tell me that he found a dollar on the sidewalk? No way. At least, not in the first ten minutes.

What he did tell me is that after school got out, he went to his locker to get his books, and then he remembered that he was supposed to pick up his sister's history book because his sister has the chicken pox and can't go to school. So Jason went back to the history class, but Mr. Roberts, the teacher, had already left, so Jason had to find the janitor and persuade him to unlock the history classroom. Then Jason didn't know which desk his sister sat in, so he had to start going through all the desks, and when he was looking in Peggy McDonald's desk, he found a love letter from Peggy to some guy in Wisconsin. With all the good-looking guys right in our own school, why would Peggy be writing a love letter to some guy in Wisconsin, of all places? Jason always thought Peggy McDonald was kind of cute, and he had planned to ask her to go to the movies with him sometime, but if she was going to act like that, he wasn't about to waste his money taking her to the movies. There were plenty of other frogs in the pond.

At about this point in Jason's story, I interrupted and asked him to get on with it and tell me what he found because I didn't have all day. He said, "I'm telling you; I'm telling you. Give me a chance." And then he picked right up where he left off. I heard about the dog who followed him from the school to Twenty-Seventh Street, and about the fire engine that almost ran into a station wagon because the driver of the station wagon didn't pull over. I even heard about the new brand of candy bar that Jason bought at the 7-Eleven. It was on sale: two for the price of one. But don't hurry on down to take advantage of this offer because the candy bar isn't any good, even at half price.

"Please, Jason," I begged, "Get to the point! You know I never buy candy bars, so quit telling me about the candy and tell me what you found."

Despite my pleading, it was another five minutes before Jason finally told me about the dollar on the sidewalk. By then, I was in such a stupor, I didn't even care.

Jason's mother always urges him to give her the condensed version of anything he wants to tell her. "Just the synopsis," she says to him. "I don't want all the details."

But with Jason, you get all the details, whether you want them or not.

I would quit listening altogether, except once in awhile, at the end of Jason's blabbering, there's something worth hearing. Like the time he called and asked if I was free Saturday afternoon. I said, "Yes. Why?" Then I heard about Jason's Uncle Harold, whose wife was in a car accident, and all about the accident, and about Harold's son, Clifford, who took a job in Hong Kong and misses out on all the family get-togethers, and Clifford's wife, Heather, who raises carp, which are huge goldfish that are worth two-hundred dollars each, and on and on and on . . . yakikty, yak,

yak, yak. But at the end, I learned that Uncle Harold gave Jason two tickets to the football game and Jason wanted me to go with him.

I did. When the players flipped the coin to see who would kick off first, Jason started telling me about the time he went to the football game with his grandfather. He was still talking at half time. Fortunately, the game was so exciting that the crowd noise drowned out Jason, which was fine with me.

#58

When I'm Sick,
I Like to be Babied

Most of the time, I value my independence. I'm eager to take responsibility for myself and to show my parents that I can get along just fine on my own. Most of the time.

When I'm sick, I like to be babied. It's comforting to lie in bed and have my mother bring me orange juice and a magazine to look at. I like it when she straightens the blanket and puts a straw in some ice water so I can sip it without sitting up straight. Sometimes she brews a special tea that smells of lemon and cinnamon and cloves. She brings me a steaming cup and the fragrance is almost better than the taste. Even if I didn't drink the tea, it would make me feel good to inhale the steam.

It isn't that I'm a hypochondriac. I would never pretend to be sick just to get attention. I don't fake illness to get out of going to school either. It's worse to have to make up a test than it is to take it with everyone else.

No, I never try to appear any sicker than I am. But when I actually do feel sick, it's always nice to have someone else who cares.

In order to fully appreciate being babied, it is necessary not to be TOO sick. When you have the stomach flu so bad you can't make it to the bathroom, and have to urp into a pan, you are beyond benefiting from your illness. You will reap the rewards of being babied only if you can anticipate a glass of 7-Up™ with pleasure, rather than gagging at the idea of putting anything in your mouth. So if you get sick, do it with discretion.

I suspect my mother likes these temporary regressions into my babyhood as much as I do. She doesn't want me to get sick, of course, but when I am, and it's clear that my problem isn't fatal, she figures she may as well make the most of it.

In my normal, well state, I wouldn't think of letting her sit on the edge of my bed and smooth the hair back from my forehead. So she does it when I'm sick.

Under ordinary circumstances, she wouldn't dream of fixing tea and toast on a tray and bringing it to me in the bedroom. If I were well, she'd tell me to get my lazy bones out of bed and sit at the table for breakfast, like the rest of the family. But when I'm sick, I ask for a tray, and enjoy the luxury of room service. She enjoys bringing it to me, and sits beside me while I eat. Sometimes she'll bring her own meal on my tray and eat there with me. A comfortable camaraderie develops when you share tea and toast in a bedroom.

These times of being babied shouldn't last too long. One day is perfect; two days are acceptable; three days is stretching it. If you overdo it, you'll spoil a good thing. By the third day, your mother will be tired of the extra work that babying you requires, and you will be bored with your bedroom. Instead of snuggling cozily under the blanket while she pats your forehead, you will want to order her to quit pawing at your hair and leave you alone. When you reach that state, you know you're well. It's time to jump out of bed and be independent again.

#59

Daddy Drinks Too Much

My daddy drinks too much. He won't admit it. If anyone ever says anything about his drinking or suggests that it's a problem, he gets angry. "I can hold my liquor as well as the next man," he says. He says it like he's bragging, as if it's a skill to be proud of.

Daddy's different when he's drinking. Meaner. Louder. He says things that he thinks are funny, only nobody else thinks they're funny, and then he laughs too loud at his own non-jokes. I get embarrassed for him when he does that. I know he's making a fool of himself and he doesn't even realize it.

He and Mama fight a lot about his drinking. Once Mama was going to leave him. I could hear them yelling at each other while she threw her clothes into a suitcase. She told him she couldn't stand it any longer. I went in their room. I felt sick to my stomach, and I was shaking because I knew Daddy would get madder still if I butted in, but I had to know what was going to happen to me. Was she going to leave me there with him or what?

"How about me?" I asked. "Are you going to take me with you or do I stay here?"

Mama stopped throwing her clothes into the suitcase and stared at me. It was like she'd never seen me before. Like she forgot all about me and suddenly, surprise! There I was.

"You can come with me," Mama said. She said it real soft; I could barely hear her.

I heard Daddy, though. He yelled loud enough for half the county to hear. He said I wasn't going anywhere, not without a court order. He said I was his kid, too, and Mama wasn't taking me away from him. If she wanted to leave, he said, that was just fine with him, but I was staying.

Mama didn't say anything. She just looked at me with

that weird expression, as if she wondered who I was. Then she started taking her clothes out of the suitcase and hanging them back in the closet.

I told her she didn't have to stay on account of me. I didn't blame her for wanting to get out of there. I told her to go ahead and leave. She didn't, though. She stayed and I never heard her threaten to leave again.

When he *isn't* drinking, Daddy's a nice guy. Other people think he's great. The neighbors. The people where he works. They think he's the All-American citizen. It's only at home that he gets so ugly. I wonder why it is that when he drinks, he takes it out on the people he's supposed to love the most?

Lots of times on television, I've seen comedy sketches that show someone who's drunk. The drunk staggers around the stage and says stupid things with his speech all slurred, and the people in the audience laugh and clap.

I never laugh. When I see a drunk person — even when I know it's just a comedian who's *pretending* to be drunk — I think about Daddy and how his drinking has spoiled everything at home.

The last thing I want to do is laugh. Being drunk isn't funny. I know. My daddy drinks too much.

#60

A Falling Star Is a Wondrous Sight

Every year, late in the summer, my family chooses one night to stay outside in the dark and watch for falling stars. The first time I was included, I was only five years old. My parents told me I got to stay up late that night, long past my usual bedtime, because we were going to sit in the back yard and look for falling stars.

It sounded great to me. At the age of five, anything which allowed me to stay up late seemed like a fine idea.

When night fell, we spread a blanket on the grass, lay down, and stared at the sky. I asked which star was going to fall and my father explained that we didn't know which one it would be, but if I watched the sky carefully, I would probably see a streak of light.

"You'll know what it is as soon as it happens," my mother promised. "A falling star is a wondrous sight."

I stared upward. I saw millions of tiny pinpoints of light all twinkling and lovely. I saw a sliver of moon, too. But I didn't see any falling stars.

"Be patient," my mother said. "Sometimes you have to wait a long time to see one."

To a five-year-old, one minute *is* a long time. I stared and stared at the sky, but when nothing happened, I looked down and began fooling with the fringe on the blanket.

Immediately, my father said, "There's one! See it?"

"Yes! Yes!" said my mother.

I jerked my eyes upward again, but I was too late. I had missed the falling star. My parents assured me there would be another one, so I began staring again, gazing with determination in the direction my father pointed. I saw nothing. My eyes grew tired from straining skyward and I closed them, just for a moment.

"Look!" my father cried.

"There's another one!" said Mother.

My eyes flew open. Too late. I resumed my vigil, determined that this time nothing would make me take my eyes off the sky, even for a fraction of a second. Nothing would have either, except a giant mosquito chose me for his dinner.

When I heard it buzzing around my ear, I shook my head and kept staring at the sky. The mosquito continued to buzz. I shook again, never taking my eyes off the stars. The mosquito slowly circled my head and then apparently decided my cheek would make a fine landing place. I heard the buzzing stop and felt the bite on my cheek. Instinctively, I swatted my face — and instinctively, I blinked.

"Oooh! Aaah!" shouted my parents. "That was a long one!" Whereupon I burst into tears and had to be put to bed.

We tried again the next year — and the year after that. It was always the same. No matter how long I stared at the sky, the falling stars only fell when I was looking in the other direction. One year I timed it. I stared upward for twenty-eight consecutive minutes and there was no action in the heavens. Not a single star chose that twenty-eight minute period to fall. But when I went inside to go to the bathroom, my brother claimed to witness not one, but four brilliant falling stars.

After that I refused to look anymore. I decided if a meteor wanted to slide out of the sky and land in my back yard, I would be glad to go out there and observe it. But if I had to watch the falling stars perform in their own territory, forget it. Since all I ever got for my efforts was a stiff neck and itchy mosquito bites, I saw no point in wasting more time. What's so great about falling stars, anyway?

And then one night, I was camping out with some friends. We lay in our sleeping bags, talking as our camp fire died out. Straight above my head, a flash of light suddenly streaked across the heavens and disappeared into the Milky Way.

"Hey!" my friend said. "Did you see the falling star?"

"Yes," I replied. "I saw it." I smiled to myself in the darkness and stared upward, hoping to see another one.

It's true. A falling star is indeed a wondrous sight.

#61

Got a Quarter I Can Have?

Got a quarter, mister? Got a quarter I can have?

I live on the street. You heard me. I'm on my own and I sleep wherever I can find a space. Sometimes I'm lucky and get one of the beds at the shelter. Sometimes one of my friends has a place to stay and lets me stay there, too. Sometimes I sleep on a park bench or, if it's raining, under the viaduct. It's dry under there and the wind isn't so strong.

Yesterday some do-gooder lady from the social service department talked to me. She asked me if I wanted her to call my parents for me — tell them that I want to come home. I told her she must be out of her tree. Life on the street ain't too hot, but it beats life at home. I wouldn't go back there if you paid me. Go back to what? Getting beat up over nothing. Watching my old man drink up his paycheck and then take it out on Ma and my sisters.

The do-gooder lady told me it's dangerous for me to live on the streets. Hell, I know that. But it was dangerous at home too. At least here I don't have to watch out for anybody except myself.

You know what makes me laugh? It's when I see ads for diet clinics and diet pills. "Lose weight fast." "Take off unwanted pounds." Hundreds of people are so overweight that they'll pay money to try to lose a few pounds, and here I am, standing on the corner, panhandling for quarters so I can get something to eat.

Most days, I'll get three — four dollars. Enough to buy a couple of burgers and a pack of ciggies. Oh, I know, I know, I shouldn't waste my money on smokes. They're bad for me and I'll die of lung cancer. Well, to tell you the truth, I don't much care. What is there for me to live for? So I can wake up, stiff and cold, and stand on the corner another day and hustle people for quarters?

A smoke makes me feel better. Calms me down. I figure it's money well spent. And it doesn't hurt anybody but me, so whose business is it?

I can tell what you're thinking. You're thinking, "I'll bet he *(She)* does drugs too. All kids who live on the street do drugs." Not me, buster. Most of the street kids *are* into drugs; but I'm not getting caught in that trap. No, sir. Drugs do bad things to your mind and my brain is all I've got. This brain has kept me from starving and from getting mugged. It's kept me out of prostitution. A lot of kids get into that because they need the money and then they can never get out. Not this kid. I'm too smart for that.

Some day this old brain of mine is going to figure a way for me to get a job and earn some real money. I'll rent me a room somewhere, the same place to go back to every night. And do you know what I'll have in that room? A bed. Yep. I'm going to buy me a bed, all my own, with warm blankets and a pillow and sheets. *Clean* sheets. And I'm going to sleep in that bed every night.

Got a quarter, mister? Got an extra quarter I can have, for food?

#62

Long Live the Easter Bunny

Even after I knew the truth about Santa Claus, I still believed in the Easter Bunny. Easter was my favorite holiday, not because of any religious significance, but because I thought there could be no greater joy and wonder in the world than the fact that a giant rabbit hopped through my house and hid colored eggs, chocolate rabbits and marshmallow chickens.

Some hiding places were traditional. I could count on finding a colored egg in the clothes dryer and another one in the oven. Other places changed from year to year. After finding an egg in the shower three years straight, I ran confidently to the bathroom, whisked aside the shower curtain and looked at nothing but the drain. The bunny had fooled me again.

I always helped dye the Easter eggs. First we put vinegar and water in custard cups and then I carefully added the tablets of color, watching as they fizzed and bubbled, stirring each one with a different spoon, to avoid mixing the colors.

Balancing the hard-cooked eggs on those little wire dippers was tricky and more than one egg landed with a *crack!* in the bottom of the custard cup.

Sometimes I tried for multicolored effects. I would hold the dipper in the dye so that only half the egg was immersed. Then, after that half dried thoroughly, I'd put the other end of the egg into a different color.

One year after all the eggs were colored, we discovered that they had not been cooked long enough. Back they all went into the pot, to be boiled for another ten minutes. The dyes all faded and ran together into a sickly grey. We had all grey eggs that year, but the Easter Bunny hid them anyway and they were still fun to find.

I was nine when my cousin, who is five years older than I,

told me there isn't any Easter Bunny. We were walking home from the corner store and I said I hoped the Easter Bunny would bring me a solid chocolate rabbit, like he did last year.

Dottie wrinkled up her nose at me. "Easter Bunny!" she said. "You don't still believe in the Easter Bunny, do you?" She made it sound like I still wet the bed or sucked my thumb.

"He came last year," I told her, but even as I said the words, I knew she was right. A sick feeling churned down deep inside me, and I bit my lip to keep the tears out of my eyes.

Dottie walked faster, as if spurred on by my stupidity. "I knew you were a nerd," she said, "but I never dreamed you would still believe in the Easter Bunny. Be logical, for once in your life. How would some giant rabbit get into everyone's house at night? Where would he get all the eggs and candy? And where would he live the rest of the year — in the zoo? Oh, I never heard anything so dumb! My baby cousin still believes in the Easter Bunny!"

Dottie ran howling home, holding her sides and laughing hysterically. I trudged into my room. I lay on the bed and thought about those glorious mornings when I raced through the house in my P.J.'s, clutching my basket and searching for red, blue and yellow eggs. I thought of the wonderful moments when I spied a chocolate rabbit, peeking at me from behind a chair or a yellow marshmallow chicken, nesting half-hidden in a house plant. Tears trickled down my cheeks and ran into my ears.

I wasn't crying because I wouldn't get any more Easter goodies. That wasn't it, at all. The truth is, I don't like hard-boiled eggs all that much, and I knew I could buy chocolate rabbits and marshmallow chickens with my allowance. No, I wasn't crying over lost candy. I wept because, even at age nine, I realized that I had lost something precious, something I would never have again. I'd lost the ability to believe the unbelievable, to trust in that which logically could not happen, but did anyway. I cried because I knew I would never again awake on Easter morning, confident that a giant rabbit had hopped through my house in the night, hiding colored eggs in the clothes dryer and chocolate rabbits behind the chairs.

That year when I went into the kitchen on Easter morning, Mom pointed to my empty Easter basket and said I'd better start hunting to see what the bunny had left me. I opened my mouth to object, but when I saw the look in Mom's eyes, nothing came out. In one of those sudden flashes of understanding, I knew that Mom was fully aware that I knew the truth. In that instant, I made a decision that would affect me for the rest of my life.

Unlike Dottie, who sees the facts and nothing more, I decided I could know the truth about the Easter Bunny and believe in him anyway.

I grabbed my basket and raced through the house, from dryer to oven to shower. I sprinted toward a marshmallow chicken that I spied on top of the refrigerator; I shouted with glee when I found a chocolate rabbit under the couch. And I realized as I ran that I will always be able to believe in the unbelievable, and to trust in the illogical. Because I knew, as I filled my basket with colored eggs, that love is stronger than logic. And as long as I choose to believe in him, there will always be an Easter Bunny.

#63

Refrigerator Art Gallery

One day in nursery school, I painted a picture. It was a large picture, filled with purple horses and giant butterflies, and a girl with hair so long that she tied it between two trees and fashioned a hammock from it so she could take a nap.

I used water colors, rinsing my brush carefully whenever I changed to a new color. It took me most of the morning to do the picture and when I was finished, I thought the painting was wonderful. I could hardly wait to take it home and show it to my mother.

Mom admired it, as she admired all my creative efforts, and then she said the painting was so pretty that she thought we should hang it up for awhile so that we could admire it longer. She took a roll of tape from the drawer and carefully taped my painting to the door of the refrigerator.

As I stood in the kitchen, munching a graham cracker, I felt the most delicious exultation. I stared at my painting, on display for all the world to see. I was proud, and satisfied, and I felt a deep desire to create another work of art which would be worthy of being taped to the refrigerator.

I know now that my mother was not the first parent to hang her kid's artwork on the fridge, nor will she be the last. But I want to go on record as saying that whoever *did* think of it first, was a genius. As that first person taped that first drawing to that first refrigerator, he or she began a family tradition which any mental health professional would be proud to claim credit for. Think how many young egos have been nurtured because parents hang finger paintings and other works of art on the refrigerator.

After my initial success, I threw myself into painting with a frenzy. I spent hours at the easel, creating fanciful new works. I painted polka-dotted barns, and houses with six chimneys so

Santa could choose whatever size he needed. Once I painted a whole chorus line of ladybugs wearing black dresses. I was offended when my nursery school teacher thought they were watermelon seeds, but my hurt feelings disappeared when I got home, because Mother taped the picture on the refrigerator. What did my teacher know? If the painting passed the refrigerator test, it must be good.

It never bothered me when old paintings were taken down and discarded, to make room for new ones. The old ones had already had their moment of glory and I always thought the newer ones were better anyway.

I finished nursery school and kindergarten and then elementary school, all the while contributing various works of art to the refrigerator door. They kept the kitchen colorful and seeing my work on display kept me eager to create more masterpieces. I wonder if Michelangelo's mother displayed his early drawings in her kitchen. Even though she died when he was just six, she may be responsible for the Sistine Chapel.

Despite the early encouragement my efforts received, I eventually realized that my artistic talent is not outstanding. Although I enjoy painting and craft work, I do not intend to study for a degree in art, nor will I pursue a career which requires creativity of that sort.

Whatever future career I have, I will be better at it because my early drawings were taped to the refrigerator. When my finger paintings were displayed, I learned that I was a capable person. I realized that if I worked hard at a task, I would be rewarded by a feeling of satisfaction for a job well done. Eventually that feeling of self-satisfaction became more important than my mother's praise.

I don't suppose a survey has ever been done on this topic, but if someone ever studies all the Pulitzer Prize winners, and the artists with one-man shows, and the musicians with gold records, I suspect the results will show that behind every creative achiever is a parent who hung drawings on the refrigerator door.

ALSO BY PEG KEHRET

Books for Young People:

Winning Monologs for Young Actors

Acting Natural

Adult Books:

Wedding Vows

About the Author

Peg Kehret enjoys a dual profession: playwright and novelist. Her funny, heart-warming plays have been produced in all 50 states and Canada, while her books for young people have earned a wide readership and critical acclaim.

Among her many honors are the PEN Center West Award in Children's Literature, the Golden Kite Award from the Society of Children's Book Writers and Illustrators, Children's Choice Awards from twenty-nine states, the Forest Roberts Playwriting Award, and the Henry Bergh Award from the ASPCA. Many of her books have been selected by the American Library Association for its Recommended Books for Reluctant Readers list. Her work has been published in Denmark, Australia, Norway, Portugal, Canada, Sweden, Scotland and India.

Peg is a widow who has two grown children and four grandchildren. She lives in Washington State where she is a volunteer for animal rescue groups. You can learn more about Peg at www.pegkehret.com.

Order Form

Meriwether Publishing Ltd.
PO Box 7710
Colorado Springs, CO 80933-7710
Phone: 800-937-5297 Fax: 719-594-9916
Website: www.meriwether.com

Please send me the following books:

_____ **Encore! More Winning Monologs for**   **$15.95**
Young Actors #BK-B144
by Peg Kehret
More honest-to-life monologs for young actors

_____ **Winning Monologs for Young Actors**   **$15.95**
#BK-B127
by Peg Kehret
Honest-to-life monologs for young actors

_____ **Acting Natural #BK-B133**   **$15.95**
by Peg Kehret
Honest-to-life monologs, dialogs and playlets for teens

_____ **Wedding Vows #BK-B151**   **$11.95**
by Peg Kehret
How to express your love in your own words

_____ **The Flip Side #BK-B221**   **$15.95**
by Heather H. Henderson
64 point-of-view monologs for teens

_____ **100 Great Monologs #BK-B276**   **$15.95**
by Rebecca Young
A collection of monologs, duologs and triologs for actors

_____ **112 Acting Games #BK-B277**   **$17.95**
by Gavin Levy
A comprehensive workbook of theatre games

These and other fine Meriwether Publishing books are available at
your local bookstore or direct from the publisher. Use the handy
order form on this page. Check our website or call for current prices.

Name: _____ e-mail: _____

Organization name: _____

Address: _____

City: _____ State: _____

Zip: _____ Phone: _____

❑ **Check Enclosed**

❑ **Visa / MasterCard / Discover #** _____

Signature: _____   Expiration
                                          date: _____ / _____
           (required for credit card orders)

Colorado residents: Please add 3% sales tax.
Shipping: Include $3.95 for the first book and 75¢ for each additional book ordered.

❑ *Please send me a copy of your complete catalog of books and plays.*

Order Form

Meriwether Publishing Ltd.
PO Box 7710
Colorado Springs, CO 80933-7710
Phone: 800-937-5297 Fax: 719-594-9916
Website: www.meriwether.com

Please send me the following books:

_____ **Encore! More Winning Monologs for**   **$15.95**
Young Actors #BK-B144
by Peg Kehret
More honest-to-life monologs for young actors

_____ **Winning Monologs for Young Actors**   **$15.95**
#BK-B127
by Peg Kehret
Honest-to-life monologs for young actors

_____ **Acting Natural #BK-B133**   **$15.95**
by Peg Kehret
Honest-to-life monologs, dialogs and playlets for teens

_____ **Wedding Vows #BK-B151**   **$11.95**
by Peg Kehret
How to express your love in your own words

_____ **The Flip Side #BK-B221**   **$15.95**
by Heather H. Henderson
64 point-of-view monologs for teens

_____ **100 Great Monologs #BK-B276**   **$15.95**
by Rebecca Young
A collection of monologs, duologs and triologs for actors

_____ **112 Acting Games #BK-B277**   **$17.95**
by Gavin Levy
A comprehensive workbook of theatre games

**These and other fine Meriwether Publishing books are available at
your local bookstore or direct from the publisher. Use the handy
order form on this page. Check our website or call for current prices.**

Name: _____ e-mail: _____

Organization name: _____

Address: _____

City: _____ State: _____

Zip: _____ Phone: _____

❑ **Check Enclosed**

❑ **Visa / MasterCard / Discover #** _____

Signature: _____ *Expiration
date:* _____ / _____
(required for credit card orders)

Colorado residents: Please add 3% sales tax.
Shipping: Include $3.95 for the first book and 75¢ for each additional book ordered.

❑ *Please send me a copy of your complete catalog of books and plays.*